# The Making

"Brian Day's *The Making* is a modern epic of the human universe—incantatory, propulsive, mesmerizing in rhythm and language, in story and myth. In this engaging and immersive read, one falls deeply under the spell of creation—the scientific wonder of the universe and the human wonder of this unique and visionary tale."

—Karl Meade, author of *doom eager*

"Be dazzled and blessed by the pantheon of religious and mythical figures who join forces with science to tell the history of the universe in Brian Day's *The Making*. His lyrical poetry makes the most of their divinely intricate narratives, weaving multifaith threads into a satisfying whole. He centers the offbeat, embodied, under-told sides of figures ranging from Vishnu and Sky-Woman to Jesus and his angel-activated mother, crafting poetry that transcends heaven and earth."

—Kittredge Cherry, author of *Jesus in Love: A Novel*

"With *The Making*, Brian Day sets himself a daunting task—to tell the story of the universe in one long poem. Astonishingly enough, he succeeds thanks to dazzling language that's both fierce and precise and an exhilarating vision that brings together Snow White and the Buddha, angels and electrons, dinosaurs and Muhammad to tell the one story, all the stories, our story. Day's teeming imagination opens our hearts as well as our minds to the interdependent wonders of our multifarious universe."

—Murray Reiss, author of *The Survival Rate of Butterflies in the Wild*

"With a unique voice, rich language, and inspired cadence, *The Making* weaves the story of the universe from 'the day biology was born' through legend and myth 'to the bowl and the birth of the stars' through the world's religions and on to the current climate crisis to find 'not hope but hope in hope's existence.' This poet is intimate with language and its power to transform words beyond words."

—Christine Smart, author of *The White Crow*

"Brian Day presses forward through the arc of the cosmos with language that's brilliantly alive. Among gods and thousands of mirrors, 'matter and story pour themselves into being.' The poet tells us that it begins with desire. We listen; we praise."

—SANDI JOHNSON, author of *The Comfort of Angels*

# The Making

A Poem

BRIAN DAY

RESOURCE *Publications* · Eugene, Oregon

THE MAKING: A POEM

Copyright © 2024 Brian Day. All rights reserved. Except for brief quotations in critical publications or reviews, no part of this book may be reproduced in any manner without prior written permission from the publisher. Write: Permissions, Wipf and Stock Publishers, 199 W. 8th Ave., Suite 3, Eugene, OR 97401.

Resource Publications
An Imprint of Wipf and Stock Publishers
199 W. 8th Ave., Suite 3
Eugene, OR 97401

www.wipfandstock.com

PAPERBACK ISBN: 978-1-6667-7947-9
HARDCOVER ISBN: 978-1-6667-7948-6
EBOOK ISBN: 978-1-6667-7949-3

# Contents

Acknowledgments xi

## One

1. Listening 3
2. The Universe Begins and Vishnu Is There 5
3. Vamana and the Cosmos Swell 7
4. Cadmus Sows Conflict 8
5. Hansel and Gretel and Electrons Find Their Way Home 10
6. Raven Plays with Snow and Stars Are Made 11
7. Chance and Necessity 13
8. Angels and Elements Climb 14
9. Bumba and a Star Erupt 16
10. The Sybil's Leaves Gather and the Sun Is Born 18
11. Pudding Is Divided and Planets Are Formed 19
12. Earth, a Baby, a Giant 20
13. Prometheus and the Earth Are Assaulted 22
14. Job and Earth Run with Sores 23
15. Moses and Guru Nanak Discover Water 24
16. Praise 26

CONTENTS

## Two

1. Listening  31
2. Life, Enlightenment  32
3. Pause  34
4. The World Is Animated by Heavenly Light  35
5. Ganesha and the Planet Find a New Way to Breathe  36
6. Narcissus and Bacteria Regard Themselves with Desire  38
7. Tiresias and the First Taste of Sex  40
8. Krishna and Cells Multiply  42
9. Raven Watches, New Creatures Appear  43
10. Sky-Woman Spreads Soil and Plants Arise  45
11. Ezekiel's Vision of Insects  48
12. Change  49
13. Aeneas and Amphibians Cross between Worlds  50
14. Eggs Are Encased as Treasure  52
15. Niobe Watches Her Progeny Erased  53
16. Praise  55

## Three

1. Listening  59
2. Joseph and Life Ascend from the Pit  60
3. Resilience  62
4. The Fisherman's Wife and Dinosaurs Obsess about More  63
5. Persephone Returns to a Brilliance of Flowers  65
6. Mary, Jesus, and the Beginnings of Mammalian Love  66
7. Baldr, Loki, and a Perfectly Aimed Extinction  68
8. Praise  70

## Four

1. Listening  73
2. Mammals Walk through Sleep and Dream of Stars  74
3. Proteus and Mammals Twist through Forms  76
4. Orpheus and the Wings of Song  78
5. Profusion  80
6. Gods Construct the Human Body  81
7. Nanasimgit Opens the World with His Knife  83
8. The Fire God Is Found in Wood  85
9. Israelites and Others Travel to a Promise  87
10. Seven Brothers Make a Team  88
11. Speech Ignites Muhammad's Mouth  90
12. David and the Soothing of Music  92
13. Jesus Is Rebuked, Art Takes Flight  93
14. Praise  94

## Five

1. Listening  99
2. Seeds Are Sown, Plants Spring Up  100
3. Circe Domesticates Animal-Men  101
4. Ganesha Splits Himself, Writing Appears  102
5. Religions Arrive with the Gifts of the Fairies  104
6. Muhammad Meets the Foreign  106
7. Odysseus and the Underworld  108
8. Story and Dream  110
9. Draupadi and the World, Stripped and Unstrippable  112
10. Praise  114

## Contents

## Six

1. Listening  117
2. Adam and Eve and the Arrival of Industry  118
3. Raven Is Reassembled with the City and the Nation  120
4. Jacob and Nations Steal a Blessing  122
5. Raven and We Find a Double Face  124
6. The Heavens Address Us and Put Us in Our Place  126
7. Becoming Ourselves  129
8. Muhammad Heals the Moon  130
9. A Tapestry Is Laid over the World  132
10. Snow White and We Keep Hankering for More  134
11. The Earth Is Threatened and We Foresee Our Destruction  136
12. Praise  141

## Seven

1. Listening  145
2. The Lost Disciples Find Their Way  147
3. Moses and We Meet the Holy World  149
4. Communion  151
5. Gautama and the Signs of Turning  152
6. Hanuman Discovers a Way to Continue  154
7. Gods Make a New Deity  156
8. Varaha Rescues the Still Beautiful Earth  158
9. Praise  160
10. Envoi  162

# Acknowledgments

I WOULD LIKE TO thank those who provided feedback on the poem: John Barton, Jennifer Morrow, Christine Smart, Murray Reiss, Karl Meade, Diana Hayes, Sandi Johnson, Rowan Percy, Susanna Jacob, Julie Glazier, Ingrid Mohr, Janet McClelland, Nedjo Rogers, and Grant Jahnke. Thanks to Bryan Young for support and patience during the years of writing.

Grateful acknowledgment is made to the following publications, in which some of these poems first appeared, some in somewhat different form or with different titles:

*Counterflow* ("Listening 7"); *Faith Today* ("The Lost Disciples Find Their Way"); *FreeFall* ("The Fisherman's Wife and Dinosaurs Obsess about More," "A Tapestry Is Laid over the World," "Snow White and We Keep Hankering for More"); *Querty* ("Hansel and Gretel and Electrons Find Their Way Home")

*One*

## 1. Listening

It begins in listening,
                        begins in wish,
begins with the sweet
                        daring pluck of desire.
It begins with us here
                        stalled and stricken,
intent on imagining
                        a story to inhabit;
and we cannot press forward
                        without turning back,
without the narration
                        of what being has been.
We venture a new
                        transcription of the cosmos,
stepping to the canto
                        where creation began;
we listen that the making
                        might be told, might continue,
that we as we chronicle
                        would not be its end.

Murmur in our ears the speech that stroked
the ribs of silence. Unspool the film:

show us what predates the human eye;
move us with a music preceding the tympanum.

Proclaim the tale that is all creation,
the serpentine stretching of everything's making;

flourish your ravishing cadenzas within us.
Rouse us that we might tell the world whole,

might face ourselves here as in epic and scripture,
in texts that pulse with what we might be.

We court creation, invite its lines,
listen for language oracular, lyric,

and ours, for a path toward some conceivable coming.
Train our ears to the notes of a newly scored covenant;

lay the narrative that tracks us from never to now.
Stitch our history back to the shadow of its stories

that knowledge might again consort with image
and with a silken love of language. Ease

as the cosmos to the slippers of poetry; recount
the making in its sweep within the temple of our ears.

## 2. The Universe Begins and Vishnu Is There

We begin with imagination blank,
    at the curtain of silence where all music hangs
    glittering. On the black eternal sea, on the floating
chaise longue of eternity's serpent, this obsidian
    cobra gifted with multiple heads and hoods,
    a smooth god reclines, his chest rises and falls:
Vishnu in the deep blue reverence of his skin.
    We can hear the silence sleeping in his eyes,
    feel the ease of his back on Sesa's smooth scales,
motion on motion, stillness on stillness,
    Vishnu on serpent, serpent on sea.
    It is the beginning for the billionth time.
Making pressed the nib of its thought to space
    and from a nothing and a never a squirming
    amorphous something was born. A pure pitch
struck through freshly minted space;
    a minim of existence was squeezed through nothing's funnel—
    a packet so miniscule it could only hold everything.
A slight smile shifts upon Vishnu's lips,
    a smirk that turns to the curve of the worlds;
    he embraces and unlaces the first breath of time;
dream slips from its moorings, drifts as
    a perfect unbegotten oneiric world; eyelids
    flicker, as matter and story pour themselves to being.
Here where darkness was everything and the brother of light,
    all the world's actors in ruck and scrum
    were crammed in one tight egg of beginning,
tugging in the womb to find and claim their parts.
    It was the starting gun of all rambunctious being,
    the A from which all harmonies erupt,
the black point of thought that will rainbow to language.
    We watch as if we stand hushed above the sleep
    of a child; we watch as if we were Vishnu's guardian,
and our eyes hold the god in fierce silent care.
    There is in us no one more tender than this vigil.
    Within this inferno of cosmic ignition,

those fiercely insensible billions of degrees:
    cool water, black serpent, blue flickering of eyelids,
    the beautiful blur of breathing and dream.

## 3. Vamana and the Cosmos Swell

At once everything bubbled into catastrophe,
    black wounds of nothingness oozing through space,
    slashing the fabric as it was woven, the cosmos
rocked by its hankering for size. When Vishnu
    is born (as he will be born untellable times)
    as the dwarf Vamana, he hides inconspicuous,
a curled snail, an embryo, within the world's womb.
    He eyes the machinations of Bali,
    the tyrant-bully demon who squeezes
the strangled worlds tight in his grip.
    Vamana, diminutive, a beggar at the feast,
    asks of the swaggering demon a boon:
that he might map out a modest pied-à-terre,
    a minute corner of the universe he could call his own.
    The space of three steps is all he asks:
three steps of a dwarf, a thing of no consequence.
    Magnanimous in imperium, Bali consents.
    Vamana cracks open the pupa of his dwarfish
form, his compacted body billowing in size,
    the midget of the village swollen to gianthood.
    He takes, as he has been granted, three steps:
this plane, middle Earth; and the depths;
    and the infinite sky. He leaves no corner
    of this wide universe beyond the reach of his toe.
There was the minuscule bud of the cosmos,
    and what had been the next thing to nothing
    broke in an instant all the rules of growth, ballooned
to the colossal, the unthinkably vast. Ventilated
    and freshly formulated space teemed
    with physical thought, yeasting the ylem
with newly invoked and invented being.
    The universe sprawled its newfound limbs.
    Vishnu as Vamana perfuses his person
through the expanse of the cosmic night,
    sweeps clear the immense and polished hall
    where the play and the dance of the worlds might begin.

## 4. Cadmus Sows Conflict

The blanket of the infant world ripped in two.
    Sudden as a lizard severing from stone
    the cosmos snapped itself into factions.
Cadmus, still heaving from the monster's conquest,
    splattered with the liquids of the virulent serpent,
    stands with a handful of the creature's teeth
like white jewels fallen from the gums of a child;
    and the silver voice we'll call Athena
    directs him to sow them to the turbulent ground.
Sword as ploughshare, he furrows and scatters,
    the countless teeth biting, sinking into soil,
    multiplying, it seems, like salt where he sows them.
He watches the earth in rippling eruption
    bloom in a crop of spear-tips and plumes,
    a tight-packed field of bronze and skin:
helmets, rugged faces, tendoned necks, brawny shoulders;
    the theatrical elevation of seeded soldiers to air;
    all the structure of torso and machinery of legs,
until their sturdy sandals stand on the ground.
    Two armies face, bear the colors of their camps:
    matter and antimatter and they were at war.
There was stuff and its matched destruction,
    matter mirrored by the weight of its own obliteration.
    They clashed in the brazen tumult of their armor,
clashed as clanging cymbals together
    in the clap of being with what would annul it.
    Filleted flesh, red swords, keening cries,
these freshly born bodies crumpling, weltering,
    soaking the soil from which they'd risen.
    The armies almost precisely matched, each
might have slaughtered the other to even extinction.
    But there slipped to the scene, from nowhere,
    from some black inscrutable bag,
a tremor of imbalance, an edge of advantage.
    What was nearly a wholesale scene of carnage,
    a corpse-strewn voiceless final scene,

was not. There was a mere hair of predilection
    for being over nothing, story over void.
    A few bright surviving soldiers stand:
the thinnest remnant, a billionth, remained:
    the filament by which our own lives hang.
    Between horizons strewn with gore,
the standing heroes survey the scene,
    know themselves charged with some founding future.
    Being, shaken, breathed, stepped forward.

## 5. Hansel and Gretel and Electrons Find Their Way Home

Those buzzing and pollinating thoughts of matter,
    that haze of chance and drift and making:
    they roamed and wandered in the tug toward home.
As the everything spread as batter and cooled,
    those bees of being we've named electrons
    made their way home to the childless nuclei,
and all by the natures of themselves accepted.
    Gretel has outwitted the dim-sighted witch;
    she and Hansel have averted their roasting
till their flesh is loosed from their bones, escaped
    that baked and blank insentient future.
    Now they bob in turns on the back of a duck,
cross the wide river that returns them to their lives.
    The bottoms of their brains are licked with sugar,
    they have wandered the long night through the black whips
of trees, and their insides shimmer with promissory light.
    The hands in their pockets and apron are blinded
    by jewels, gloved with wonders of a hundred colors.
Through the lattice of branches they sight
    their house flashing freshly before them,
    render it larger with each eager step,
all the weariness that weights their young limbs
    rinsed by the vision and scents of table and bed,
    of their father who appears at the door to embrace them.
Atoms. They are the phonemes of the cosmic kerygma,
    form a unit as basic as family, hearth,
    that tiny adhering self-orbiting sphere,
a structure rhymed, relaxed, and rounded.
    Within their ingenuous symmetrical faces
    waits all the making of biology, brain.
With atoms' compaction, light was granted passage:
    a scribbling of signature white onto space—
    light quick and live as a fish on a line.

## 6. Raven Plays with Snow and Stars Are Made

Raven flies black through the black of space,
    through the void and the falling of what has always been,
    through the swirling thick restlessness of snow.
Here before the beginning it is snowing,
    and Raven is alone in the world of snow.
    White powder settles softly on his wings,
flake upon flake comes to rest on his back,
    and Raven rolls in the glide of his flight—
    the angling of his course through directionless dark.
A nubbin tumbles across his back,
    grows to a marble, a fruit, a ball,
    in that habit of whiteness sticking to itself.
He builds it in the sportive rhythm of creation,
    dipping and lifting as newness rides
    across the broad span of his wings, as it
collects and assembles the white of space.
    Then that quick fillip, that exuberant toss,
    flicking the ball to seek its own fortunes,
to travel wherever his impulse has sent it.
    Raven watches in sly delight
    as this whim of his motion swells in size,
drawing a body of snow to itself:
    this burgeoning globe his play has begun,
    a bright eye white against night's black wing.
The drifting dandelion fluff of the universe,
    the floating, unaccented grains of thought:
    there was only this, ungrammared.
Now a miracle of unevenness, a slight
    clustering here, an allowance of space, atoms
    clumped like tears in flour, like ribs and veins:
ridges, tributaries, rivers welted on the map
    of the sky. The streeling bits of being
    acquiesced to gravity's discreet introduction,
met and discovered a company's warmth:
    cold dust collecting like kids on a playground,
    like curious tourists drawn to a juggler.

There was a blessed gathering in,
    a holy compaction of wide-scattered ash,
    matter grabbing at its memory of density,
reveling in some new frisson and friction,
    jostling and sticking and flinting new light,
    roaring and flaming itself into mane.
A star ignited, a broad forest of stars.
    In one snap the cosmos shook out its blanket of light,
    set a billion parallel kingdoms;
did this in play, in exquisite artistry—
    the gorgeous pouring of swirling milk,
    whorls of coral, amethyst, liquid egg.

## 7. Chance and Necessity

We're born of this dalliance of chaos and cosmos,
this unlikely, elusive calibration of the random.
This universe, unknowable in its future and all
traceable back to one inexhaustible impulse—
is strangely at home at the tables of gaming,
in the darting between the numbers that are cast:

adapting to every new swerve of its history;
smoothing the fabric of each discovery,
and mending every frayed edge to story. It
pursues the glinting oneiric image that scuds
from nowhere into its eyes; the plots lured
to the planes of its perennially thirsting skin.

It is as if it is always morning, and all that is
is shooed out to play in the wilds of time.
The universe watches—thrilled, aghast—as fresh
unlikeliness sweeps in boldly before it,
as sciences unroll the floor where it dances,
and it slips into steps it had not foreseen.

And who is this wily crafting from accident,
this ebullient bricolage from stochastic rubble—
there digging deep in the sandbox of creation?
Who is this playfully dexterous and inventive
diablerie that gambols sensuous, light-footed,
through the field of its fiercely imagined desire?

Who is this dazzling gymnastic display,
this marvel of nimbleness, mystery of agility?
Perhaps some primal wish for wonder,
a faithfulness vacant of any omniscience;
a bating of breath in the listening to story;
a daredevil consent to imminent surprise.

## 8. Angels and Elements Climb

Now the long unaccountable introspection of stars,
    their turning eyes inward toward burning cores,
    compressing in alchemy all they'd collected.
Here the fulgent metabolism of matter
    into something akin to a musical scale,
    and also, lavishly, fiercely, into light.
Atoms exulted, clapped their hands in jubilation
    as the cosmos tinkered with its chemistry set,
    forged ornate jewelry in abstruse alembic;
as that roaring inferno began its work,
    shapes moving within those leapings of flame
    as svelte young men in a tyrant's furnace,
the torches of their bodies steady, uncowed,
    mouths issuing bright coronas of song.
    Atoms, florescent, surged through their growth spurt,
hurling themselves to the bigger, the bolder,
    in the rising pitch where new matter is proclaimed.
    They listened, these motes, these modes of being,
to the rungs they climbed and formed from fire,
    listened as purely as covenants of angels
    ascend their luminous ladders to heaven,
feet mounting the requisite steps of the sky,
    fingers tingling at the touch of molten gold.
    On these scales and staircases through the supernal,
the ethereal chemical steps of ascent,
    the angels climb sturdily from light to light,
    in a fire no human mind could hide behind.
Voracious in the hunger, the transmutation
    of their hearts, they—the angels, the atoms,
    the impulses to rise—trip readily up
the chromatic of elements, calling each of these novel
    orders by name: helium, lithium . . .
    carbon, nitrogen, oxygen, fluorine . . .
silicon, phosphorus, sulfur, chlorine . . .
    titanium, vanadium, chromium, manganese:
    names simple and abstruse as the taxa of angels.

Here new form of atom is new order of song,
    new setting of the one primeval alleluia,
    new structure complex in mechanics of parts.
They play their hopscotch up the grid of elements,
    configuring from what is most widely granted
    all the needful materials of the world.
They make it up to where a door is shut
    resolutely before them. Iron. Recalcitrant.
    No angel can lift their feet one more rung.

## 9. Bumba and a Star Erupt

A star is a listening for the sforzando of its death,
    the bestowal of its accumulated treasures to space;
    a magnanimous dying waiting to arrive.
Angels stretch to reach beyond the top rung of the ladder,
    waver, seek for something beyond them.
    They leap in something akin to suicide,
a sacred, savage immolation of themselves.
    In the beginning are Bumba and the dead
    wet world. When his time, the god's time,
has come, nausea rises bilious in Bumba's belly.
    There surges the impulsion to be rid of what
    swells inside him, and he knows no comfort
as he writhes in his flesh. He suffers the great
    emetic of creation, the dyspepsia, this sick
    when world emerges tugged from the roots of his tongue.
The star cracked its singular seedpod of light,
    ripped open its innards in rich visceral sacrifice,
    explosion of bowels and raw exposed organs.
It held not a mote of itself in reserve, jettisoned
    all it had carried and cared for, geysered out
    everything in utter vastation, disgorging,
propelling as threnody its wide canticles of light.
    Bumba's guts extrude themselves into air,
    the glove of his gullet everted into light,
and he heaves up the bodily filth of creation—
    the glistening, birth-slick, internal oils,
    the spread spectrum of raw and raucous light.
What Bumba vomits first is sun,
    a ball to heat and dry the damp world.
    A further nausea, a further revolt,
and there follows leopard, slimed and patterned,
    its Argus eyes of fur. There follows
    the dome, the probing of the tortoise, the one
who is born already ancient. There follow
    heave after heave in the sick that will not cease:
    all the fish that flicker in the mind,

the crocodile fringed with uncountable teeth,
    the white heron standing clean as a beacon.
    From these will proceed the making of the world.

## 10. The Sybil's Leaves Gather and the Sun Is Born

There in the shambles of her cave sits the sibyl,
    strewn about her a forest of fallen leaves,
    each one inscribed with one isolate word.
The particles of language have come unclicked,
    meaning by maelstrom swept into havoc.
    The once-stellar motes floated lightless, unpinned,
listened, frigid, for the memory of heat.
    Then, in the breath of the turning of stars,
    half-articulate gravity murmured the name
of each maundering bit. A group of congeners
    clustered, rubbed shoulders; and what was aphasic,
    dismembered, lisped toward form. There arose
from the cold refuse strewn from stars,
    from the fine grains that drifted residual from stories,
    the wish for a light where they might be warmed.
The sibyl devotes herself to the motion
    that shuffles the leaves toward conjured meaning,
    this crisp and cryptic riddling of the world.
To all eyes but hers they are mere wreckage;
    her sight is the ether that grants their significance,
    drawing from broken words rough grammar.
Always there is breeze, the erratic,
    the whiffling of words to oracular pattern,
    the confluence of syllables toward some future.
The lexical fragments gather in her vision;
    the leaves of the atoms puzzled together,
    agglomerated as the start of a novel star;
invented, remembered the semantics of light.
    The hearts of matter were squeezed to fresh fire.
    And the sun was lit in the lamp of the sky.

**11. Pudding Is Divided and Planets Are Formed**

And there were miasmic clouds of dust,
    a squid's ink exuded from the making of the sun.
    Swirls of color amassed from mist,
and these clouds found their numbered centers
    of gravity, compressing, and spinning as spheres:
    a rarity of planets plucked like pearls
from the sea, their invisible pathways compassed
    on space. So at the time of the birth of Rama,
    as Vishnu readies for another plunge into time
and King Dasaratha beseeches the divine
    to slip into his family, a brilliant white horse
    is caparisoned, paraded, pampered on sweets.
It is sacrificed with precise invocations:
    picking with tongues the cosmos's treasury.
    There with his feet in the darkening embers
stands the crimson-clad bearer of the gods,
    fresh as the turn of another clean page.
    In his hands a bowl of gold with a silver lid;
in that bowl, the sumptuous blue pudding of impregnation.
    Dasaratha's wives all kneel to receive it,
    spoonfuls of smooth pudding given, shared.
They submit to know azure spread over their tongues,
    to have this sweet glory exalt their mouths,
    brim and animate the caverns inside them.
The god-seed is divided among the wives,
    divided again to twins within their wombs,
    meted and fractioned in precise degrees.
The sun's seed was portioned to the fraternity of planets,
    granting to each some tranche of lineage,
    some particular basking in their god-father's gaze.
The women taste the sweet semen of godhead,
    the host that will grow to blue sons inside them:
    the greatest the one who will swell to Rama.

## 12. Earth, a Baby, a Giant

There compacted a sphere, third from the sun:
    a chunk of rock, unpromising, rough,
        the gangue, it seemed, of some richer business.
A chain of gold held it bangled about
    the sun's wrist. Heat was forged
        by its elements' decay, its body sheathed
in a silk of flame; and it turned
    that our evening and morning might begin.
    Earth was tossed about the sun—an egg
careening in chilly indifferent space.
    What floats is embryo, is fetus slick
        with the fluids of albumen and slumber,
with a fervid wish for the world to begin.
    In the egg is Pangu, the boy concealed
        within the Earth: a bead, a baby,
the infant stirring pith of a planet.
    The child of a ten-thousand-year gestation,
        curled and contained in the calyx of himself,
bobbing, adrift in a galaxy's bulrushes,
    he is Earth's first loneliness for beauty.
    There cracks open the moment when he can be born:
he casts off his nutshell, stretches vast compacted
    limbs: stands, a man, a giant;
        stands, perplexed, aggrieved, on this land.
This world is not the one he's imagined,
    does not bear that brightness of scarlet and blue
        but muzzes itself with what is not distinct,
is gray on gray, unbrushed with color.
    He thirsts for dense hues he carries
        from sleep: landscape as dreamscape,
inhabited, whole. He wills a finer
    order of creation, a saturated beauty,
        earth settled below him, sky pressed above,
a holding of the riotous elements in place.
    He tamps with his feet what will become home,
        sculls and sweeps the chapeled ceiling of sky;

braced like Atlas in creation of space.
    For years he separates, holds world to its form;
    and then his dying creeps toward him.
He hurls his death at the thirsting world,
    flings his dreams over grayscale Earth
    as he bequeaths his corpse to the planet:
muscles to soil and blood to seas,
    bones to the jagged line of high mountains.
    He exudes as some men do the odor of miracle.
Beauty is what he has breathed as his mantra,
    beauty and color, color and dream.
    This he bestows on the planet that bore him.

## 13. Prometheus and the Earth Are Assaulted

Manacled to stone, Prometheus writhes,
    a worm sacrificial in a fierceness of heat.
    His life is this tide of torment, and he rides
the long trough between strike and strike,
    the repeated silver scissors of invasion.
    The eagle, that plunging minister of vengeance,
pierces the smoothness, the sheath of his skin,
    rives again the cage, the branches of his ribs, gouges
    out the cowled bundle of his liver, its sleek
and vascular heft. Day after day
    it is savagely the same, the ripping
    at the intricate spiderwork of veins. Prometheus
weathers this precise unvaried repetition:
    the predictable, annihilating pain. There is nothing
    but the shadow and the coming of the shadow that stuns
the one sky of his mind with pain.
    Earth was a sore misshapen victim,
    unable to dodge the relentless attacks.
It was strafed by shot that burst its flesh,
    fists that forced their way to its viscera, poxed
    its body with oozing wounds, meteors
that punctured and pummeled its skin. The kludge
    of everything space had to spare, Earth
    was alloyed and imbued with impurities, with the refuse
of treasures it would hold in its stores. It birthed
    the moon, that waif of scarred light,
    a face floating open-mouthed, appalled.

## 14. Job and Earth Run with Sores

Job sits in the chafe and itching injustice
    of irredeemable pain. He sits in the tent
    of pus that once was his skin, his raw
flesh cratering, all nude and new,
    his insides excreting and glossing his skin.
    His bones corrode within the sac of himself
and his every nerve begs for scraping with sherds.
    Earth was a woeful suppurating mass:
    it welled with blood, erupted with boils,
extruded a fury of liquid stone:
    the flailing red rage of a planet convulsing.
    Land was candescent with its festering wounds,
a roiling of liquids without sign of redemption;
    heaving its molten organs to its surface
    and draping its viscera over its skin.

## 15. Moses and Guru Nanak Discover Water

Moses, in the savage drought of the wilderness,
    battered by derision, contempt, complaint,
    obeys the absurd commandment of his God
and strikes his staff to desert stone. Up
    springs that holy dream of water, the clear
    liquid metal, the brilliant generous gushing
shine. Liquid is loosed from concealment
    in stone. The planet's blistering temperature
    fell, landscape cooled, eased toward solidity,
and from within the cavernous chest of Earth
    there shot up shouts of steam and song:
    water leapt in miraculous ascent, lifted
its fingered hands in praise, and summoned
    a firmament of water: masses of rampant cloud,
    a heaving gray pressing its breast to the land
and breeding the imaginary creatures of the sky.
    The sluice gate of the clouds swung wide,
    rain was invented as harp-strings of silver,
and air was blessed with sheets of descent.
    Water wept to hear itself spoken.
    Rock was laved in its first glass of wet,
there poured year after year of munificent rain,
    brimming the bowl of the ocean's floor.
    Earth was spread with fluid fields,
with surge of tide and swell of wave,
    was marbled in blue and swirling white.
    Here on the ocean were Sesa, Vishnu,
floating where they have always been.
    Guru Nanak, enwombed in the river of his bathing,
    springs up like a drop that falls to the sky,
ascends without loss from world to world,
    from firmament to whole and unbroken firmament.
    His clear body drips with the marvel of oneness;
a seamless circling of every thing to itself. He
    knows water as the opening note of this world;
    his body is lit with its bright circulation.

He sings the world he holds unsundered,
    opens with his one purling voice
    the pour of this wild spigot of joy.
Water rose and water fell
    and water was its own direction.
    And Earth was wedded to sky with this ring.

## 16. Praise

Our daily lives have been tracked back
to all that is primordial, seminal, in creation:
the shaking out of the first folded sheets of mirabilia.

We have been here from the first crack of history,
find we have no course to take but praise:
the thirsting in our throats to exalt this making,

extol the profuse innominate cosmos.
Praise the abiding first scene of story:
the suspension of Vishnu and Sesa on sea,

the breathing and the dream where the fecund begins,
the inception of matter, emergence of motion,
the irruption of wonders in the tale's first breath.

Praise the pyrotechnic pollination of void,
the swelling and striding and claiming of space;
the soldiers springing from scattered teeth,

the edging of being over sheer absence;
the wish that leads the lost children home,
the gathering of matter to bright jewels of family.

Praise Raven's slyness slicing through sky,
his gathering the scattered to roundness of form,
the ignition of the first illumination of stars;

the marvels of impulse in the field of the determined,
the bewildering enmeshment of pattern and chance.
Praise the stars in their fabulous manufacture of light,

the ascent of matter up its own waiting rungs,
its twirling in debutante violet and rose.
Praise the holy emetic dispersal of grains,

the eruption of elements from Bumba's guts;
the gathering and auguring of prophetic leaves,
the sun that centers our listening lives.

Praise the ritual invitation of god into bodies,
the sharing of the bounteous blue pudding of heaven,
the parure of planets encircling our star.

Praise the stirring within this one egg of Earth,
the gestation of a giant in inchoate wildness,
the fierce wish of a dreamer for an answering world.

Praise the plucking of liver, eruption of skin,
the pummeling of meteors, spewing of magma.
And the rise of a planet with the promise of water:

the revelation of spring and pool and rain,
the flash of sun on the lips of the waves,
the pleasure of its light in a thirsting mouth.

*Two*

## 1. Listening

And now there came a hush, a hiatus,
a waiting of the water draped on this world.

Earth attended to its nascent story,
inclined its ear toward some coming—

as a postulant would yield to receive a dream:
listening toward that allurement of image,

that faint and breathy susurrus of future.
The heart of the world lay angelically

open, the body of the waters lifted and fell;
and there within water, a wish that making

might utter some brilliance barely conceivable,
fashion from dreamscraps a marvel of becoming;

that on this expectantly spinning planet
would flower the patulous profusion of creation.

Earth listened in patience to a stirring invitation,
an imminence that gathered and glimmered and dreamed.

## 2. Life, Enlightenment

Among the velleities teeming in the sea,
    there began experiments, concocting, tom
    cookery with ingredients lurking in the cupboards.
There, in the depths of unplumbable oceans,
    were the vents, the geysers of chthonic forces,
    the fervid exhalations from the planet's forges.
Frigid dark water was branded with heat,
    in the Ginnungagap of all creativity,
    and there began the chemical courtship of contraries.
Among spindling towers of old white gold
    the unknown addled itself into being:
    matter wizarded as by lightning into species,
breaking open the code the cosmos set within it.
    Now a magic that brightened the universe's eyes,
    a marvelous being that lived and wiggled
and conceived more being, spiriting its likeness
    forward into story, into silkenness of dream,
    this stirring toward near-infinite flourishing.
There appeared the masterwork we'd christen bacteria,
    this pointillist scheme of minuscule life.
    It was the day biology was born.
A brilliant new color had been invented,
    one as pure as yellow or red.
    And the one who was not sleeping awoke.
It was a beginning as singular as the Buddha's,
    a night from which time itself might be tracked.
    He seats himself beneath the spreading branches of a bodhi,
lowers himself one evening as Gautama,
    and a Buddha of beauty cracks open his skull
    in that clap when flowers release themselves to scent.
Worlds pour through hidden membrane to his being;
    he is plunged to an ocean that would not ever
    consent to drown him. A star steps into a drop
of water; the sun rises crimson inside him.
    A universe sweeps through and illumines the one
    he had been. His mind is now that flush of poetry

where every instance brims to all—
    and he knows each one smoothly in the bowl of the mind,
    the gift of their deep dark and wonder.
The entire pantheon takes their seats
    as exuberant fans in a coliseum, arrays
    themselves tightly on the horizon of this breaking
being, petals falling from the opening
    fists of the gods. Life is invented,
    incanted, bestowed, in this unlatching of dream
cached in dream. It is a magnanimous moment of origin,
    a conception, incarnation, of immeasurable potential,
    and nothing that Earth would have known to pray for.
Stars peered to the petri dish of this planet,
    where afloat on the ocean's silver paten
    squirmed the seeds of all unfinished making.

## 3. Pause

And then a fermata, indefinitely held;
    stillness and stillness, suspension of story,
    the respite from this exhaustion of novelty.
Bacteria made no move, no progress,
    simply spread in the body of the sea.
    There was a listening for the pattern of water,
bacteria, blank. They could not rush
    the stewing of incipient thoughts inside them:
    floating and milling and staring at the sun.

## 4. The World Is Animated by Heavenly Light

A posse of photons threaded their way
    through the needle's eye, found the precisely
    devised shapes of bacteria; the supernal
slipped into aquatic flesh, and sunlight ignited
    every nerve of their lives. The tiny floating lifebuoys
    were ravished by the effulgent one they gazed on,
sunlight astounding the shape of their lives, transforming
    all they knew to bright sugar, whole oceans invested
    with the rippling of sweet. Their fibers thirsted
like wool to be drenched in sweet green,
    and they were lit with the dazzling speech of conversion,
    this novelty coursing from their kindling selves.
The survivors of Jesus huddle abject
    in a small hidden room. They have known
    all the wonders they are ever likely to know,
and the sacred has been lifted from the table of their lives.
    There alight on this unexceptional morning
    flames that illumine each woman and man,
that are at once wind and fire and anointing—
    a battering brilliance swirling from nowhere;
    a breath that ravishes the caverns of their lungs.
They're hurled toward some tearing rapture
    where they're doused with light and force and glory—
    where they are molten, profuse, unrestrained,
white with every lightning strike of language.
    They are gloved in the liquid skin of angels, charged
    with a refulgence their forebears never named,
afflatus flowing in cadence and phrase.
    Their mouths are glazed with unlearned speech
    that pours like aureate honey from their tongues.
God-talk recasts the shape of their palates,
    bridges the meniscus of image and word
    in this fluid, forking gift of grace.
Each coin of them rings with the day's jubilation,
    their every organ lit with the brilliant, this
    lacework of fire that sets their fields ablaze.

## 5. Ganesha and the Planet Find a New Way to Breathe

As they learned to tear water into edible parts,
    feeding on hydrogen, bacteria spewed oxygen
    into the atmosphere; found the reinvented
air unbreathable; choked and withered
    on their own repellant pollution, peered down
    the short tunnel of their extinction.
Shiva's wife Parvati, too often left alone,
    fashions from her own scurf after bathing
    a boy who becomes her son Ganesha.
When Shiva returns from his ascetic labors,
    he finds a brazen impudent kid
    barring his path to his own bathing wife.
Shiva, peremptory, orders him to move;
    the boy won't budge, and the god, unaccustomed
    to refusal, draws his sword and severs the boy's
soft neck. Shiva stands over the decapitated
    boy. Parvati appears, takes in the scene, swells
    to a rainstorm of bereavement, castigation, harangues
her husband, pummels him with words, wails
    that he has murdered the blessing of her days,
    keens at the ground-soaking stump of her son.
Shiva, god of ashes, lord of death,
    stumbles in silence to the grove of his remorse.
    Lying in the forest: a young sleeping elephant.
With his sword still wet with human blood,
    he hacks off its head, lifts it, pliant
    trunk and flapping ears, carries it home,
affixes it godwise on Ganesha's shoulders.
    Shiva grafts the impossible onto the world,
    and Ganesha finds himself filled with a sinuous
breathing, a mammoth intake of air.
    And there among bacteria a marvelous reversal;
    there appeared a swift magician's trick,
pulling life from the black silk hat of death.
    A switch was flipped, the poison alchemized
    into elixir, roomfuls of straw swiftly spun

into gold. Tiny bacterial lives were refashioned:
    they jinked away from the death that faced them,
    invented a wilder way of breathing,
a nimbleness averting an imminent ending.
    They thrived on the oxygen they had unleashed,
    were nourished by the gutterly grace of existence.
Life gasped at the moment of its resuscitation;
    Ganesha stands refreshed inside his second life—
    the dear swaying god who sweeps away obstacles.

## 6. Narcissus and Bacteria Regard Themselves with Desire

Narcissus leans over the glass of the pool,
    and here within the water's face—
    beatitude, consummation, the entire unbroken
body of beauty, the answer to his own brimming
    desire. He is suspended, transfixed in attraction,
    pierced by the transverberation of love,
that hummingbird sipping of self within self.
    He craves immersion in his own face—
    to be lost and drowned and bright with breath;
he wishes, with the force of his keen body's longing,
    to be what he is and adore what he is; to be
    burdened by no need to choose between them.
He would be the whole religious body of water,
    know himself hover and plunge and be caressed,
    while still the hand that delights in caressing.
He cannot relinquish his vision unfingered—
    that further alluring encapsulate world,
    the teeming freedom inside his own flesh.
Narcissus would at once be film and forgetting—
    pervaded with himself, expanded, exalted—
    sweet with the wish of his own smooth skin.
Bacteria, breeding new forms from minor
    mutations, multiplied themselves, flirted;
    cell gazed into cell, yearned for new union,
desiring the taste of each other, the taste
    of themselves, desiring unborderment, immersion,
    release; to know themselves in half-foreign flesh.
One body slipped breathlessly into another
    to vanquish, surrender, be suspended within it;
    know itself reordered in the moment of admission.
Yielding to the seminal cellular ecstatic
    and spun with hieroglyphic webs of code,
    it lived with indulgence within its host:
beings of mirror, beings of pane,
    laced in wanting, wantonness, desire,
    in this rite of predation where no one was lost.

Coupled and complex within their one skin,
    they were the singular and plural of the world,
    became eukaryotes, a blind breach of order.
They were deliquescent, exultant, denamed,
    cell fusing itself with its answering image:
    abandoned, recast, and deep inside themselves.

## 7. Tiresias and the First Taste of Sex

The floating world felt a further frisson of desire,
    and what was teeming and infinitesimal
    ferreted its way toward the secret of sex.
*Meiosis*, someone whispered in a corridor of sea,
    and the others lit up in all of their ears,
    anticipating glistening on the surface of their lives.
Desire for another bit into the cells;
    they yearned to touch, border to violable border,
    and pleasure was embraced as creation's new consort.
When Tiresias, out for a solitary stroll,
    spies the runic coupling serpents
    constructing the lubricious double helix of their forms,
he strikes his staff at their brazen entwinement.
    His strike at the snakes strikes back at him,
    triggers a lurching enantiodromia.
Tiresias is hurled to quick metamorphosis,
    transformed by his impulsive assault on sex, skids
    across the threshold of gender: his body,
his place and perspective radically revised.
    Ductile, he'll be serially male and female
    and male, probe with his tongue both forks of pleasure,
taste life and lust on each side of that flummoxing
    divide, his innards and inclinations twisting and
    twining as sinuous snakes. He will be the carnal
shaman, the psychopomp of sex; and
    he will be the seer, the counselor of heroes,
    the one to peer lucidly into the future.
Creature was tugged to otherness of creature;
    there began the irresistible striptease of genes,
    unzipping and marrying their ribbons of code,
rubbing two colors to myriad tones.
    Sex and death arrived sheathed as twins,
    the mortal concealed beneath the greatcoat of desire.
Tiresias is entered by, dipped in another,
    learns the timbres and modes in which the body sings,
    becomes the bright gauge of sexual delight.

He moves with the ease of androgynous angels
    as they slip through blessedly eloquent bodies.
    All that had been single was laced with lust.
The seas clapped their hands at the birth of such play;
    there began the great masque of the sacred licentious,
    night crackling with the bridgeable distance of love.

## 8. Krishna and Cells Multiply

Night. A clearing in the forest. The air dense,
    electric, blackest blue. Every woman of Vrindavan
    has been roused by the notes of Krishna's flute,
pulled from the depths of a hungering sleep; and now
    they run pell-mell down the trails to this forest
    shrine. Krishna shapes his lovely moue,
and the flautist flaunts his undulant body.
    The women, the gopis, stand circled and eager
    for the dance, their bodies brushed with silvery longing.
Each one yearns to be Krishna's one partner,
    to merge with him in the sway of adoration.
    Krishna cannot shoulder their numbered disappointments,
cannot choose only one, leave the others bereft.
    He cuts, deals himself like a fresh deck of cards,
    effects his own sleek multiplication;
refracts, kaleidoscopes, to all that there is—
    poised in his ever so tactile flesh
    before the adoring eyes of each one.
He is himself—singular, profuse—
    the incarnate answer to their every wish—
    and they each hold Krishna solely in their arms.
And now in that menagerie of simple cells,
    that profligate array of innovated shapes,
    there arose again the wish for more.
Abecedarians heard notes on the air,
    were lured toward a marvel they could not conceive.
    One became the center of many adorations,
cells pressing to and compounding with cells,
    smitten and swirling as some composite being,
    where the single is transfused into multiple bodies.
The marvelous multi-celled figures danced
    in their fluid miraculous synchronous motion,
    generously fulfilling the wishes of the world.

## 9. Raven Watches, New Creatures Appear

Raven is alert each morning for surprise.
    He spies an anomaly beached on the rocks:
    a clamshell broader than the span of his wings.
He readies himself to be entertained.
    From its gummy grainy slit
    peek timorous wide-eyed homunculus faces,
gargoyles stinking with curious fear.
    There is in the air a smack of smegma.
    Raven eyes the tiny totem faces:
this is the best story he's heard in long memory.
    Raven lures the craven creatures,
    works the smooth voice he'd affect
to coax imbecile or snail. These skittish
    bedraggled dwarves are insuppressibly inquisitive,
    and the first clam-juiced little man emerges
with his grainy nakedness, his meager little waggler;
    a second, then another, crawl from the shell—
    all quivering and cowering and spooked by the breeze:
soil-brown, sumptuous, slick as fish,
    carved with ridges of native muscle.
    Their bodies swim out into the world.
Soon they are capering, gaming on the rocks,
    agog in their air-licked bodily selves,
    rippling in fingers, toes, and torsos,
their fluid incessant reshaping of faces,
    the oscillations of delight and disappointment—ablaze
    with this world they've shucked themselves to explore.
And now the first plates of visible forms,
    this Wunderkammer that invites our fascinated gaze:
    everywhere in ocean a carnival of costumes,
a taroting of cards in arcane order.
    Through the undulant forests of algae
    we step through the gates of an aquatic city
where citizens of refinement conduct their ornate lives.
    Here are the elegant coral-colored vases
    of sponges, ribbed and stellate and sensate

to all that rinses over their lives; here
    are lamp-like sacs of filmy light, their motions
    of investiture, censer, oblation, figures of nimbus
and milky embrace; here are those nobles
    flaunting carnelian and cornflower blue,
    who have wrapped tender bodies in carbonate shields,
who swan in the shapes of tiny twisted hats,
    of scalloped, veined, and feathered fans.
    Here is the elegant imbricate tribolate
collecting on crystals precious slivers of light,
    receiving the world it scuttles and skirts through.
    Here millipede dragons feathered with down,
the unearthly five-eyed opabinia, its proboscis
    nuzzling at the fruits of the sea. And now
    the careful crafting of backbone, threading
each vertebra to a rhyme scheme of spine,
    and inventing the lush visual symphony of fish.
    A white ladder reached from tail to blossoming brain
as fish found the litheness and liberty of swimming.
    Hansel lays a trail of silver pebbles
    that glint like pearls in the rays of the moon.
With the profligate caprice of created forms,
    Earth was lavishly, extravagantly clothed,
    the envy of all its craning siblings.

## 10. Sky-Woman Spreads Soil and Plants Arise

Bare stone dreamed the cool covering of soil.
    The land was buffeted, strafed and needled
    by the strike of rain; water wore grains
of stone from their sleep; wind in its insistence
    brushed a powder from land. At the prospect
    of abundant plates of rock, bacteria
reshaped themselves to the hunger of fungus,
    edged thin lives over the lip of the land,
    soft mouths cutting toothless through the skin of stone,
eating their way through fields of rock.
    Behind them they left the detritus of the fertile,
    stone shedding scurf so something might be made.
And again in the universe's patterned tale
    there were fine grains of dust imbued with hope.
    They received the minute lapping waste
of the living and the dead, composed the precious
    heredity of soil that holds the memory,
    the iterative work of the circle of the earth.
A woman lives in cloud-land, walks on white,
    is bold to discover why she's been forbidden
    to dig at the roots of the towering tree
that stands like a taunt at the center of her days.
    She is daring, digs, spies water
    far below her, and gazing, dazzled, bemused, loses balance,
tumbles, clutches at the tree's low branches,
    fingers finding no purchase but shearing
    dark seeds. She falls without knowledge
of what sphere rocks below her, sky-diving
    down toward the inhabited waters of the world.
    The animals below—loon, otter, beaver,
muskrat, toad—they smell her danger,
    muster in an instant a scheme to save her.
    They scramble as they can, and quickly there swoop
the paired solicitous loons who break
    her fall on the sleek oiled swingseat
    of their meeting wings, and set her

down on the geographic back of the turtle
    who floats there, a setting thirsting for a story.
    The sky-woman needs some cushioning comfort,
softness of soil. One by one the animals,
    muskrat and beaver and ardent otter,
    descend to the deep surrounding waters
to retrieve from the lightless bottom the barest
    scrap of it; attempt and fail, all spluttering
    up to the surface with bodies all but
collapsed and with no merest offering of earth.
    And the little toad, the toothless, incompetent,
    dives down and down through that far crushing deep
to a darkness that etches primal terrors on his eyes,
    that squeezes all but one last pocket of hope
    from his lungs. He scrabbles up gasping, three-quarters dead,
a small nugget of soil lodged inside his mouth.
    With her finger the sky-woman carefully
    scoops out the dirt. It is brown and rich
and smells of life. She smears it over
    the turtle shell, smooths it with her palm,
    until it covers the whole broad dome.
It receives with perfect gentleness her feet,
    in the snowiness of footfall she knows from the clouds.
    From her other hand she slips to the soil
the seeds of the sky-tree, scatters them over
    the turtle's vast shell, over all the curving
    fertile Earth. There sprouts the lavishness of green,
of trees and their fruits in their every season;
    and the woman, fallen, has found her home.
    From the veils of emerald at the fringes of the sea
the pilgrim plants stepped cautiously to land,
    staked their tentative claim to shore,
    their territory advancing in a shawl of green,
in the gingerly creeping of liverworts and mosses,
    the flourishing of resolute fronds and horsetails.
    They took what they knew of the languages of light,
learned the trick of holding water in the heart,
    the mechanics of some sweet further green meaning.
    They twisted solar history to terrestrial life,

perfuming the air with the ether of oxygen;
> grew electric in unquenchable thirst for the sun,
> with leaves the fresh green of young angels' wings.

Stems discovered the lignin of trees,
> learned the chemistry to purchase their height—
> and Earth arose in its luminous cape of green.

Plants dispersed themselves in pollen, seed, and spore,
> prostrated themselves in the ritual of death,
> bequeathing their bodies to the furtherance of soil.

## 11. Ezekiel's Vision of Insects

As the land unfurled its lush invitation,
    sea creatures listened with hunger and trembling,
    emerged from the rocking black of the ocean,
hurled themselves out and clung to land;
    found solidity beneath incipient feet,
    mastered the airy mechanics of breath,
poured themselves forward to unclaimed space.
    They learned to live in the lavish leaves,
    to leap and suspend themselves on air,
extending the dreamlike gauze of wings.
    Here was the skirr of a further revelation:
    the living lightning of insects soaring
through a vault that still exceeded them, sailing
    as wind and spirit carried them, spelling
    the spontaneous wonderment of flight
and inscribing the first divine letters on air.
    With the manifold wings and the voluble unwearying
    mouths of angels, insects were that hectic,
triumphant, incessant, profuse in their praise.
    In their multitude was the rumble of mighty waters.
    The whirling chimerical creatures glimpsed
by Ezekiel, they flaunted the sheen, the tremor,
    the rippling, scintillation, brashness of bronze,
    the flow and honeyed heat of amber.
They steered their fierce bright vehicles of flame,
    bearing the coals, the embers of their forging,
    the polish of wheeling iridescent geometries—
sparkling with every sharp color of ice,
    their chips of sapphire chiseling the sky.
    They faced at once in every direction;
and their eyes, that glittering clockwork, spun,
    gyred, swiveled as wheel within wheel,
    kaleidoscoped the colors of the great given world.
Crafted of lapis, topaz, emerald,
    of all of the stones that studded the sky,
    they were brooches pinned to the flesh of the air.

## 12. Change

Who's to account for this curious, prolific,
illimitable universe that does not dully
repeat itself, let every day
be one of rest; that does not quietly
set down its pen, stare out the window,
but returns to its manifold labors each morning?

The universe is nothing but its indigenous magic,
its restive wish to reshape what it is,
elaborating the compacted impulses of its origin
and expanding these into melodic lines—
not one note but this single unbroken song.
There is only this liturgy of unveiling the new,

this intimate antennaed groping of matter,
extending some track lightly etched on the moment
before, tongue tracing a rumor of sweetness on air.
At each crossroads the cosmos veers to the voluptuous;
aspires to speak what has not yet been uttered—
is a tale that at core craves solely itself.

## 13. Aeneas and Amphibians Cross between Worlds

And again among the denizens of ocean
    there stirred a wish to transgress the threshold
    of sea. There was bubbling in the muck and at
the murk of the verges. There was again
    a wish for some new means of breathing,
    for bodies reordered in their respiring cores.
A new thought crept across a page of the brain:
    of breathing in that drowning element
    where the world that forbade them opened its arms.
A face peeked above the still surface of water—
    a fish, a transitional fish, an amphibian;
    a stumbler with fins becoming feet;
an unthing; a half-lunged, half-footed creature
    that hauled itself on stumps up weed-slimed rocks.
    This one, this team of pioneers, invented
a doubleness of breath, of gills and lungs:
    turning the world several clicks of the compass,
    flesh lanced and renamed and made spacious with air.
These mercreatures clung to the edges of wet;
    lured by the smorgasbord of insects before them,
    that tantalizing banquet draped to the horizon.
The ears of Aeneas have tremored with the news
    of that secret transporting bough of gold.
    It has glistened before him in sibyl's breath,
in memory of dream and dream beneath dream.
    Its leaves are as much his own as his eyelids,
    the bough embossed in fire on his brain.
The bearer of the bough, the sibyl has incanted,
    may pass and return through the turnstile of death.
    Aeneas knows that he from his birth
is the one cast as its bearer, glides
    through the auroral stillness of the forest,
    and there, alluring, unmistakable, pristine,
radiant as dreamlight—the bough. And it
    in courtesy extends itself toward him.
    He holds the golden ticket of transgression,

the charter that unlatches a barred and guarded world.
    It is given to him to be this liminal figure,
        to know the shades pouring their wisdom to his ears.
The gatekeepers, unsurprised, nod at Aeneas;
    wave him in to this dim, penumbral light,
    admit him as if he were not himself.
Eyes playing at the film between the worlds,
    he strides with a gasp to now-breathable air,
    steps with fleshed feet to Elysian fields.

## 14. Eggs Are Encased as Treasure

A poor man, a man of teetering future,
    digs in his turnip field one ordinary morning,
    scrapes his spade against what is not rock
but chest, quickens his shoveling, his breath,
    unearths the coffer, hefts it awkwardly up
    into daylight; and in one slow second, with the lifting
of the lid, the flash of all that brash gold fortune—
    the snapping of his day to an unknown attention.
    There dawns some sudden interior sun,
and his meager life is blessed with redemption:
    these coins translatable to the particulars of wish,
    and he is blessed by what springs from the dark roots of Earth,
what cracks open to light. He is a man hatched.
    He basks in the bright coruscant treasure,
    the thrill of this new gland in his brain,
and nothing can make him a poor man again.
    We arrive at another worksite of creation,
    where crews are inventing the terrestrial egg
that encases water within a small sphere,
    carrying a packed ocean to the dry of the land.
    The unborn feed from the yellow-gold yolk,
shelled and shielded from desiccation and death;
    and what has incubated breaks to slick life.
    Reptiles spread as settlers further from shore,
gowned with new film of imbricate mail,
    with supple, taut, impermeable armor.
    Hermetic, esurient, clever of tongue.
An ornate Euclidean panoply of skin.
    Wet yellows, bold scarlets, ravening blacks.
    The stained glass of bodies recounting lit scripture.
Turtles with meticulous bas-relief domes;
    the thrilling quick-curving river of snakes;
    the scenting, alert, ancestral lizards.
The Earth was zipped in resplendent flesh,
    a pouring of pigment and pattern and pride,
    the land again granted gratuitous beauty.

## 15. Niobe Watches Her Progeny Erased

Eructations of subterranean gases
    burst from volcanoes and bubbled through the sea.
    Methane disgorged itself into the atmosphere,
carbon dioxide flooded, stunned the air,
    and what had been breathable was dense
    with the rotten egg stench of hydrogen sulfide.
Landscape was grayed by falling ash.
    Temperatures soared, could not find descent.
    Water traded oxygen for acid.
Its equations fractured, all life stumbled.
    Plankton, faltering, collapsed in the seas,
    corals in all their colors fading,
ocean's nuggets and filaments forsaken,
    bibelots of its kingdoms falling from its fingers.
    Fish, thirsting for oxygen, sweltered, drowned,
their torrent of silver thinned to a sliver;
    sharks diminished, cinched to near nothing.
    The green of the world was shaven, stripped;
forests shriveled, caustic rain burning trees
    to rust. Air was wiped of insectal life,
    species whittled and plucked to near breaking.
The lumbering inhabitants of land were slaughtered
    as heat was rammed down suffocating throats
    and life skated within sight of its own annihilation.
Niobe is blessed with a full set of progeny:
    seven daughters and seven sons,
    each unblemished in face, in figure and physique.
Niobe vaunts that she must be
    the envy of every pathetic goddess,
    none of whom boasts such an exemplary womb—
least of all that pitiable Latona the women race to honor,
    risibly given a mere pair of offspring.
    Gods do not look with kindness on such words.
Latona sends her two sons with a lesson in humility:
    archers with faultless Olympian aim
    to wipe Niobe's children, her pride, from the Earth.

With the repeated ping of their bows, arrows are driven
    through windpipe, feathers flutter in throat.
    One's lung is punctured, a spluttering balloon,
another lies swamped and ribboned in intestinal wreckage.
    Arrow clatters through teeth and jaw,
    pinning to silence the eloquent tongue,
skulls pierced and granted a third eye of blood.
    One strike dispatches two oiled wrestlers
    who grapple together; in a heap they fall
in slick and slackened embrace.
    Brothers and sisters are scythed down as they flee,
    bullseyed in the point between blades of their backs.
Riders are struck while galloping away from their deaths,
    slump and tumble from the steeds they ride.
    The gods enact the relentless revenge for an arrogance
that never stained her children's mouths,
    the names they have carried now cleaned from the world.
    Niobe mantles over her one remaining child,
begs that only this last daughter be spared
    as her final child goes limp in her arms.
    Each corridor of her story has been blocked.
All within her that was blood and coursing
    is thickened, weighted, hardened to stone.
    Black metastasizes through all she is,
her entire being sinter-smooth,
    shimmering perpetually with her tears:
    the breathless weeping of death-black stone.

## 16. Praise

Praise the arrival of radiant surprise,
the abundant Buddha-life that surges to the world,
bacteria blessed with fresh animation.

Praise the beings, ecstatic, that feast on sunlight,
their anointing by swift descending tongues
of flame. Praise the supple ingenious

reinvention of breath, the grinning respiration
of a decapitated, bleeding, moribund world.
Praise that life, enamored, gazes on and is

entranced with itself, adding its body
to the floating image it thirsts to join.
Praise the twisting twining snakes

that double and divide in erotic elisions,
the gracious glide between the sexes.
Praise the circling and gathering in dancing devotion,

the multiplication of what remains one,
the ardent courtship of aggregate cells;
the opening of the lavish shell of the seas—

the curious, greasy, multi-faced creatures,
the petit-point workings of artful exactitude,
the muscular flicking kinesthetic joy.

Praise the heavenly woman who plummets
from cloud-land, the precious mouthful of soil,
the creeping of green over newly sown land.

Praise the jeweled insectal life,
the intricate breeding of brooch and bedazzlement;
the inscription of matter with impetus to change,

the fluid metamorphosis of flesh and tale.
Praise the golden bough, the breach of border,
the signal amphibian creep to land,

the entry to a welcoming doubleness of world.
Praise the golden ball of reptilian life,
the luck of discovering interred treasure,

the scattering of pigment in the clambering over land.
Then the hitting of the door that is closed against praise:
the keening lament that still rings in our ears,

the rinsing from Earth of elaborate family,
the erasure of thousands of trails of creation,
the slick of tears on sleek dark stone.

*Three*

## 1. Listening

Earth carted through ashes the hopes of a cosmos,
listened from the stripping of all it had been,

listened in grief and black exile from itself;
listened with its meager and manged extant species,

in penury of plant and fish and flesh.
It listened from the charnel that was the land;

listened from every worn groove of history.
It waited at this puzzling juncture of story,

as if music were there beyond its hearing—
some brightness, effusion, hidden by horizon.

It lay curled with some wish for the story to go on;
listened as if thirst might conjure new water.

Animals, depleted, listened to their inkling
for growth, listened in fiercely imagined resilience,

in slow discernment of cryptic invitation,
of a map emerging faintly from their flesh.

They listened with the ravaged corpus of Earth
for the zeal of future to be written on their skin.

## 2. Joseph and Life Ascend from the Pit

Ask Joseph: it's not a matter of fondness or deserving;
    it's not about soft spots in the cosmos's heart.
  There he sprawls bruised at the bottom of the pit,
beaten and forsaken by all of his brothers,
    the coat of bright colors ripped from his back.
  Disinterested traveling merchants find him,
take him as they would take a lame goat.
    He's no longer anyone's favored son,
    just another body on a caravan's course. But his
is a mind minutely tuned to the frequency of dreams,
    that reads images as easily as merchants read coins.
  He's privy to the code by which mysteries are ordered,
swims across the weir of worlds,
    passes like an angel through that wall in the brain.
    Fluent in symbol, Joseph knows
what it means when seven fat cows rise
    from the river, when they are followed by seven
    gaunt, emaciated, nearly dead,
when the thin ones preposterously consume the fat.
  He decrypts the pharaoh's dream, and this is all
    it takes to save a kingdom, to stay starvation;
to win release from the dungeon—and copious reward.
    Vice-pharaonic robes—silken, sybaritic—now
    adorn his flesh. Preferred organs are offered to him
at every feast. He is, by the grace of his brothers'
    betrayal, their envy and calumny, their rumors and spitting,
    their fists to his gut and kicks to his back,
their stripping of the peacock glory of his clothes—
    perched at a height he could not have foreseen.
    From a dry well he's ascended a staircase of dreams.
Speak with a tenth of your lexicon intact.
    Paint with a poverty of colors in your hand.
    Sing when almost every note has been stolen.
There were survivors and they were numbered,
    all but ground by the teeth of a ruthless apocalypse.
    The remnants huddled and skulked and survived,

creeping on a sparse depauperate planet.
>Earth hibernated through successive millennia,
>sustaining itself on what it remembered,
what it retained of the palette of its dreams.
>Creatures drifted with a saurian somnolence,
>established themselves in an alien land;
reworked the thin fine mesh of this world,
>reembroidering the fabric of their inheritance,
>their decimation painstakingly parlayed to ascent.
They found a dream track that launched them forward,
>propelled them to where they were given new clothing,
>new powers, new ease of maneuvering through world.
They were resilient, were recipients of blessing,
>characters who slip to the groove of a story,
>figures who receive the revelation of dream.

### 3. Resilience

What is the source of Earth's quirk of resilience,
its litheness in pivoting in unblazed directions:
sorting unhurriedly through untried options;
alighting on, delighting in, incipient species;
this steady inclination to risk renewal,
persist in its proclivities to regeneration?

When light retreats beneath the soil
and hope has decomposed beyond any use,
the old ones rouse themselves, meet in a circle,
confer on where some further line might appear.
They sift through the middens and detritus of extinction,
reread ancient grimoires, alchemical texts,

listen for the dreams that have not yet pressed
themselves into the world. They lave and dress
the corpse of the crucified, sing to it the late
benedictions of love, and its skin still shines
with beleaguered colors. They commence, again,
this spreading and bating of reliquary wings,

this procession of bodies to a river of light.
They listen to lore that is laden with the ancient,
to the relicts that persist in terrestrial memory;
and they know this is a world of surge and sundering,
of swell and descent of chest and dream,
of paths that vine through the rubble of loss.

History, the sister practice of prayer,
bears a fertile, unfounded hope for the coming,
an unstinting forgiveness of all that has been.
The decrepit is lifted toward the transfigured,
each discarded note finds its place in song,
each word rubbed wrongly now eased into poem.

## 4. The Fisherman's Wife and Dinosaurs Obsess about More

As she sits in the humble hut of her life,
    the fisherman's wife always hungers for more.
    She has driven her husband out again to the swells
that he might procure a favor from the fish:
    *Flounder, flounder, in the sea,*
    *Come, I pray you, here to me.*
The fish-king, iridescent, with his circlet of gold,
    grants her serial aggressive requests
    through her husband's abashed, apologetic proxy:
*For my wife, my Isabil,*
    *wills not as I'd have her will.*
    She climbs in shrill avarice the staircase of power,
lusting for whatever hangs tantalizing
    just out of reach. She ascends from the position
    of fishwifely stature to townswoman, noble,
king, and emperor (discarding the gender
    that does not serve her well in her ascent),
    trading in whatever dull status she's gained—
worn to tin as soon as it's held in her hands.
    She fumes with her ever-aggrandizing wishes—
    and next she is seated as pope, shining
in unequalled solar resplendence: in gold-
    threaded vestments studded with diamonds,
    with servants that teem as ants about her,
and commands that resound to the corners of the Earth.
    She teeters with the weight of her gleaming triple crown,
    on the three-mile-high throne where she is pinnacled.
There is, it seems, nowhere higher to reach.
    For a sleepless night she crashes against
    the ceiling of ambition until just before dawn
she discovers a greed that aspires to the divine.
    She orders her husband to return to the flounder:
    she will not be content until she can command
the sun to rise, to arc and set,
    dictate the track and phases of the moon,
    order at her whim the circling of the spheres.

Reptiles brewed in an alembic bubbling with oxygen.
    Their bodies, burgeoning, grew enraptured by size,
        could not find the perfect point of enough.
Great docile digesters of leaf into limb,
    armed and esurient rapacious predators,
        they crafted bodies ever more complex, baroque:
bodies like Achilles's dipped in protection,
    blood-thirst ripping like fame-thirst through flesh.
        Chimeras were drawn by unrestrained hands:
patterned plates thorning down the line of spine;
    multiple rhinoceros horns of defense; the mace
        of tails brandished menacing in air; coiffed and pomaded
headdresses of bone, the frill of high collars in vain display.
    They indulged in feats of obsessive musculation,
        the amassing of bodily armor and armament.
Reptiles slipped grinning to the oceans, stretching
    sinuous serpentine necks, paddles like wings,
        jaws barbed with serried triangulate teeth—
Leviathans that haunt the aquatics of dreams.
    Others leapt and shrieked through air, scurrying
        and flapping in great feathery capes; invented,
from earthly labyrinth, flight. Contraptions
    of pliable parchment, umbrella-like skin,
        they cranked their bony bodies into air.
Animals were insatiably obsessed with size:
    more, they kept demanding, more: make me huger,
        more fantastic than anything that has ever been.
Make me more than I have ever dreamed of,
    more than I was when I woke this morning.
    Make me greater, make me divine.

## 5. Persephone Returns to a Brilliance of Flowers

The nuances of nebulae, the spectra of stars,
    the pastels of sunsets and fishes' skin
    enfleshed themselves in a wonder of petals,
distilling and conceiving delicate flowers
    from all the mass and sea of green. Interred
    in the chthonic world, in dimmest penumbra,
Persephone is starved of every vital color,
    turns in the faint mineral glow of remembrance.
    She is the one who has fallen out of time.
And there comes the bewildering day her release
    is announced. She ascends, somnambulant,
    to the interrupted world, where she is lit
with the complement of all her months of darkness.
    Demeter, the motherly atrophied body of Earth,
    embraces her dried abducted daughter,
releases monochrome life to return to the fruitful.
    There opens with her arms a new hymnal of color,
    a way for fields to peal their own beauty.
Plants were decked in their lush invitational palette,
    painterly colors erupting from the earth:
    daffodil yellow, egg-yolk orange,
a poppy brilliance saturate as blood,
    that perfect, long-yearned-for cornflower blue,
    the vinous violet that quenches thirsting sight.
Flowers emerged half-curtained, unclothed themselves,
    wafting perfumes and spreading robes
    of finery to entice the sweet hovering prince.
Insects exulted in intoxicant fragrance that surfeited
    the senses, drifted in indulgent promiscuous bliss;
    the flaunting blossoms knew themselves cunningly,
gorgeously plundered, their every wish and succession
    attained. Where Persephone steps is riotous color,
    sumptuous unveiling, florescent excess.

## 6. Mary, Jesus, and the Beginnings of Mammalian Love

Sheltered in a stable of dense animal odors,
    her colorless clothing indistinct from straw,
    Mary lies emptied, exhausted by birth,
muses on the nothings poured into her ear,
    the angel-speech that entered her and is now
    tucked neatly to this packet of flesh.
She holds her ordinary miraculous child,
    spies the maze of ordeal and exaltation before him,
    holds this savior wrapped like a piglet in its slime.
She recalls that interloping stranger—
    foreign, cryptic, seductive, angelic—
    the words he spun like a ribbon of light for this boy.
Mary has humbly done what the great world asks
    (the world, the stranger—who's to discern?),
    has done what her body in that moment and this
knows surely how to do. She holds a squirming
    wet infant in her arms. Breast and mouth
    are clamped in hunger and elemental love.
It is her body, raw instinct, and love.
    It turns her within constellations of wonder.
    There is no life less exceptional than hers.
Beneath the thundering epic of dinosaurs,
    small creatures scurried at the bottom of the page,
    hid themselves in burrows, raced in their hearts.
Timidly, hidden, they bore young that emerged
    lightly clothed in lanugo—not quite
    reptilian, filmed with fur. Their newborns began
a curious licking, a seeking at the not-yet-
    teats of their mothers, an anticipatory tasting
    of salt, in that swelling of pores toward mammary glands,
the blooming of a body to bonds of attachment.
    And there on a small pink unsurprised tongue
    that first sweet sip of mother's milk:
this nuzzling and sucking, this flow of warmth—
    the invention, sotto voce, of maternal adoration,
    filial affection. No one observing these

mouse-like minor players would suspect them
    of seeding a revolution, a shift in history.
    And the shrew nods her head to the mother of Jesus.
Mary feeds her hungry son on milk,
    on starlight, on what her body has conceived
    for this birth. A flutter of angels
lights her eyes, the aureole of her skin.
    Her body is struck rock, bright spring,
    is where a new world will be cradled and nursed.

## 7. Baldr, Loki, and a Perfectly Aimed Extinction

In the god-land of Asgard, Baldr had dreams:
    Baldr, the paragon, the flower of the gods.
  Night after night he was dragged into terror;
his visions savaged him, stole joy from his days:
    these skull-guests that he had never invited.
  Dreams plunged him down to the rankness of Niflheim,
and he knew, he had seen it with his own appalled
    half-melting eyes—that in the ordure of the underworld
    a deathbed was being readied, marked with his name.
He was a god, the purest of the gods.
    The queen of Asgard listened to his dreams,
    black worms, mustered herself to protect her son,
determined to seal up every line of defense,
    prohibit every being and nameable substance on Earth
    from enacting the death that Baldr foresaw.
Frigg extracted a vow from each giant and dwarf,
    each elf and monster, each thing that she
    deemed capable of harm: vows from water
and rock and fire; a vow from each species
    of animal and tree; from every creature and element in all
    the nine worlds, that they would refuse
to do damage to Baldr. Loki, that persistent
    restlessness inclining to malice; Loki,
    shapeshifter, in the form of a hobbling old woman,
asks Frigg if any in the worlds have not spoken
    their vow of protection for the god of light.
  Just one plant, the small benign mistletoe,
vining gracefully about the oak's trunk,
    that Frigg in passing deemed too slight to do harm.
  Loki detects the crack in the spell,
crafts a dart of mistletoe, hones it acutely
    beneath his blade. In the great hall of Gladsheim
    the other gods, discovering Baldr invulnerable,
indulge in the sport of attacking what cannot
    be destroyed, hurling at him all that has vowed
    never to wound him: stones and arrows

falling neutered, smiling, at his feet.
    Baldr's blind brother Hod sits dejected,
    unable to aim, outside the bright circle
of the gods' game. Loki places
    a light dart in Hod's hand: a small one and balanced
    and sharp as a hornet. Loki draws back Hod's hand.
Hod propels what the god of mischief has made.
    A tiny dart of mistletoe, an invulnerable body—
    what are the chances of such a collision?
Flung from somewhere far among the stars
    a meteor aimed itself precisely at Earth.
    It fell through the length of a summer's day,
smashed the solar plexus of the planet,
    a pointed stake plunging to the root
    of an eye with that boiling and gurgling and bubbling
of blood. Earth reeled: its guts gaped open;
    it heaved up raw volcanic innards;
    the rivering of blood, the rain that hissed
and dripped with venom. Wildfires raged,
    the skin of the Earth was lit like a glove;
    there came the bitter blackening of the sun,
the planet dulled to indefinite twilight.
    It was as if light might lose its mobility,
    as if photosynthesis might be unlearned.
All the immense dinosaurs yielded their lives;
    the fiercest hunters in the seas were erased,
    every major player swept from the stage,
skeletons scattered like unstrung pearls.
    The dart pierces the chinks of Baldr's
    spelled armor, finds the hair-thin
gap between the worlds' pledges,
    and what was unkillable now buckles in death,
    the finest of the gods a perfect white corpse.
There is in Gladsheim a fierce swell of silence.
    There begins a grief that will outlive the gods.
    The noblest of all their number is extinguished.

## 8. Praise

Praise all mythic and marvelous things,
the eons of bold polymorphous play;
the spectacular bewildering ascent of the exile,

the gift of speaking the language of dreams,
each dexterous flourishing cadged from defeat,
the dreaming of future over filaments of loss.

Praise this robust and resolute cosmos
that artfully redeems the relicts of destruction;
the stretching years of aggrandizement and grandeur,

the wishes indulged by that munificent fish,
the bristling bravado of brawn and armature,
the extension to the nth of lizardly forms.

Praise the wanding of Earth to vernal colors,
the springing of Persephone to Demeter's embrace,
the floral exuberance of a world freshly lit.

Praise the first sketched icon of madonna and child,
the entry of a bright new order of animals,
the warmth of the maternal, familial, humane,

this commonplace appearance of weirdness and wonder.
And again, in a silence of praise, catastrophe:
the momentum of that fatal meteor, dart,

guided by blind incandescent chance,
and the inconsolable lament of the gods,
the keening with the sphere of the Earth in flames.

*Four*

## 1. Listening

Sluice yourself through
                the cracks in our hearing;
trace the way forward
                through the dark of our mouths;
narrate the creation
                that still lies before us,
the labyrinth that leads us
                from dart-strike to now.
Double again
                the helix that we've stripped
in the telling of holy
                material history:
open the scripture of our one
                precious cosmos;
stitch the glamour of stories
                back onto the world.
Let us be the cold
                starlit night of listening;
let us be the reverence
                where poetry proceeds.
Be here in every
                ovation of our breath.

The beleaguered remnant, that pith of history,
listened to the sere and death-stunned land,

listened to the rumblings of the plundered world,
listened as body to the growth of bone.

It carried all the world could hurl forward—
a stumbling messenger bearing ravaged news.

It listened from beneath the shroud of its life
for some deft and dazzling legerdemain;

listened to the incipient still drumming in its blood,
and wished the original wish of more.

## 2. Mammals Walk through Sleep and Dream of Stars

And here a breathless suspension of time
    as the prince, admitted by the parting briars,
    gorgeous in rife and crimson bloom, drifts
through the still and sleeping castle,
    each footfall hushed by a century of dust.
He passes through the absence of mandolin, madrigal,
wades through rooms glutinous with dreams,
    where bodies lie abandoned like unfolded clothes
    and the fires slumber like the pausing of stars.
He creeps through the mindless black sleep of flies,
    through the bounding abundant dreams of the dogs;
    steps through the museum of his own heart.
Steeped in irresolvable silence, this
    intricate waxwork mausoleum of wishes, he
    forgets that human voices have rung in his ears.
Tiny furred animals huddled in their hollows,
    holding lingering history in shivering paws.
    They roamed terrain thickly carcassed with death,
scavenging the meager means of survival,
    the meekest and smallest inheriting the Earth.
    These ones least favored to form a new world
slipped through a narrow fissure between eras,
    subsisted, endured, did not yield to extinction,
    lurched toward a story they could not
sense the end of, treasured and hoped
    some distant day to break open the extravagance,
    the champagne that they held cached in their genes.
The God-voice is not prone to reason,
    wants simply to pull another coup de théâtre
    out of its bag. When God announces to Abraham
and Sarah in God's most histrionic voice
    his scheme to invent a great people from their
    expended bodies, from those who are wilted
in their gonads and desires—his trick of ribboning
    the future from the patently sterile—Abraham
    is bedazzled by the sight of his teeming inheritance:

he's the guest of honor beneath the whitened sky
    of his own future, that profusion of stars,
    the near-infinite scattering of his seed across the Earth.
And Sarah's is the only apt response
    in the face of such fantasy, mockery of promise:
    laughing in her heart at the folly of God.

### 3. Proteus and Mammals Twist through Forms

Mammals cracked open the cases of their reserve;
    their tightly wound potentials sprang over the land.
    Name by name the numberless creatures were made,
the thousand slow folktales of each species' invention,
    the maps of fur and tail and paw, the release
    of every latched and aspiring kind in a flurry
of dense Ovidian episodes: enfleshing
    proclivities in opuses of limb and pelage,
    forging new wonders from wish and phantasm,
from relentless attention to the places they lived—
    till they fit to every cranny of the planet,
    pouring as light pours to brim vacant space.
Frame the jagged lines of the tiger's fur,
    sweep through days within the bulk of the whale,
    inhabit the bolt of the gazelle's acceleration,
spring with the kangaroo's tensile force,
    navigate with the bat the screaming blindness of air,
    with the monkey discover the world fit to your grip.
Now the time-lapsed elongation of limbs,
    the lupine extension of canine and craving,
    the thickening against cold of bruinish pelt,
the glut of stunningly adept adaptations,
    the concocting of a ferocious fireworks of flesh,
    an Eden that would take a near-eternity to name.
There on the treacherous greasy rocks,
    cloaked within the stink and flensed skin
    of seal, Menelaus lies waiting to catch
in his grip the fleeting of beasts, track it
    like river, lightning, tale. He waits
    with his men for the Old Man of the Sea,
the keeper and shepherd of the half-human seals.
    And when that old swimmer has beached himself,
    exhausted, on the rocks, Menelaus seizes
Proteus, seizes the fantastic name of transformation,
    grasps him by his muscled gyring flesh,
    this one body willed to almost unfollowable forms,

the convulsions that storm and assault Menelaus
    before he can affix their names, no second
    to adjust his hands to his thoughts—just these
quicksilver changes that leave his mind molten,
    his fingers abraded, stinging with burn—that gaping
    pink and glistening white, the lion with its mouth
insatiable as death, the rippling scales, the length
    and distributed viciousness of serpent that pours
    through his fingers, the furious flesh, the leopard
lithe in its wrestling, its pits of darkness,
    the tusks, the boar that will gore his body
    into furrows, the slick and muscled ropes
of water, their pacts and alliances, the hard limbs,
    the tree thrashing its centuries of strength, the figures
    of flame that deceive and demon in his hands. Present
to this epileptic cascade of creatures, this bestiary
    riffling its racing pages before him,
    his task is only to not let Proteus slip
his grip, to be the undaunted prehensile
    holder to forms, to be tenacious
    in clutching liquid time in his fists.

## 4. Orpheus and the Wings of Song

Skimming beneath the threshold of extinction
    and adorning saurian integument with feathers,
    surviving small dinosaurs veered further toward birds.
They lit on the lightness of bone to fly,
    forelegs learned to grip the air, to sail
    through blue and dimensioned skies.
Their wings announced a breach of the possible;
    uplift fanned itself to a plethora of plumage;
    syrinxes chose the modes and the notes of their scales,
the timbre, tessitura of each emerging voice.
    Arriving in a benison of exuberant excess,
    they swaddled in birdsong the newness of morning;
blackbirds dipped wings to the red of prayer.
    There entered the extravagance of toucan and manikin,
    bird of paradise, tanager, and finch,
hues of dense and painterly purity;
    shamanic bodies passing between realms,
    drawing back into daylight the life that was lost.
Orpheus slips through the watery mirror between worlds,
    his image silvered on each side of the glass.
    He pitches his tent in the deepest pit of grief,
from chthonic darkness lifts cerulean song,
    the ravishing appeal of notes gorgeous with wound.
    He will not permit his anguish to be stanched.
On the flint of his bereavement music strikes
    and flares; colors blaze fiercely where blackness
    should forbid them. Impelled by the scarlet
need of his song, he ascends on every bright
    wing of beauty, lifts grief from dim suffering
    to luminous lament. He knows keen feathers
fletched to his words, follows the air-ripping
    arc of his music; and an ungrieving future
    blazes supernal in some niche of his mind.
He stretches in song the full wingspan of spirit,
    casts from bowels of Earth toward unceilinged sky
    the plea and aspiration to ascent, rouses

each rapt deity with this yearning of voice.
   Orpheus is as magnanimous as a morning chorus,
   is as shriven and radiant with promissory light.

### 5. Profusion

Why is this universe so bent on profusion—
why the uncountable trillions of stars,
the furnaces that fashion whole rows of elements,
archipelagos of planets instead of just one?
Why the curious press to speciation,
the blazoning of making as the name of all this?

Why is what is so pregnant with excess,
the *this too and this*, the harlequin indulgence?
Why through all the reaches and fractals of the known
this faint disequilibrium inciting invention,
this strange inclination to meet and indulge
every craving for bizarreness and beauty?

How has such plenitude come to be?
If by chance, then some species of chance
overflowing with the generous: some prince
born once in a thousand generations,
a hero replete with luck and summonable
riches. In lieu of some placid order

—extravagance: this ignition, velocity, crackling
with light, this whirling Catherine wheel
of becoming—this profligate craving for the untasted,
this probing of every cranny of the possible, this
desire for the irruption, florescence of the novel—
this desire to be numbered with the number of stars.

## 6. Gods Construct the Human Body

There were stirrings within the secret chambers of flesh,
    ripplings across the tall grass of the story,
    and what would be human glided toward us.
Forest apes clustered in family and troop,
    eating and mating and cradling young.
    They held the vibration at the base of a xylophone's
spine, and the head in a querying of vertebrae
    rose from the ground; they teetered, wobbled,
    as toddlers begin to balance on two feet,
their bodies unfolding in arboreal light.
    Their eyes were lifted to scan a far horizon,
    and savannah invented the loping hominid step.
Feathered Serpent, Maker, and Heart of Sky
    conspire to form new creatures to praise them:
    minds that will shine like votive oil,
voices that redound to their makers' honor.
    They who are God embark on their work,
    and first they model bodies from mud,
but the angles will not lock and the bones do not hold.
    The creatures take no firmness, heads face the wrong way:
    awkward, askew, and best abandoned:
too weak to hold the imprint of the holy.
    The gods concede the first of their failures,
    release the muck to blur and brown the water.
And the creators, undaunted, return to their work.
    Next they fashion creatures formally human,
    carve them from firm and buoyant wood,
and these puppets mimic gesture, language,
    but cradle no spark, thrum with no hearts
    to animate their voices; their solidity will not
soften into thought. These unhearted
    mannequins are left chattering in trees.
    Hands, freed from walking, learned
the complex configuration of fingers and thumbs,
    acquired a finesse of feeling, precision
    of touch. The body was articulate, marionetted

onto brain, and the intricate intimate network
    between them developed in neural skeins.
    The sumptuous fatty flesh of prey
fed the coiling gray growth of cortex.
    The enlarging uterus molded to the movement
    toward wider craniums, more detailed maps.
The pelvis grew, bred wider, wiser,
    more sapient eyes, an altricial childhood.
    In the great renovation of hominid brains
there came the splaying of ramulose social relations,
    the further modulations of the mammalian heart.
    The gods return to the table of their workshop,
continue their patient practice of revision,
    continue to seek what they have imagined,
    what will hold an answering, devotional gaze.
God seeks the counsel of animal advisors—
    mountain cat, coyote, parrot, crow;
    shapes forms from white and yellow corn,
from what is malleable, nourishing, firm.
    The creations shine with a light that suggests
    perfection, are adept in perception and praise,
exude the unmistakable scent of the gods—
    but are inclined to veer from their author's intentions.
    Feathered Serpent, Maker, and Heart of Sky
are not entirely content or at ease;
    the beginnings of frowns now tug at their mouths.
    But their work is done: this will do.

## 7. Nanasimgit Opens the World with His Knife

They learned to extend the features of their bodies,
    appending to their limbs a predator's claws,
    its teeth, the needles and knives of its armory;
made the scrapers and blades that sharpened their hands,
    cleaned flesh from fur, shaved rock into shards.
    They came to create a culture of tools.
They learned that they could reshape the bones
    of Earth, that these were ductile, subject
    to their wills. Slow bodies took speed
in the song of the spear, exulted in the glide through the
    whistling air—their weapons and prayers
    piercing animal flesh and giving their mouths a new
magnitude of meat. They steered long hours
    to shaping stone, learned to live ever more
    in forethought, edged a further advantage on their domain.
Nanasimgit walks the road beneath the sea,
    the long road stretching out like his fortune.
    Nanasimgit the hunter walks with his knife,
an instrument as dear to him as his name.
    And a goose who stands waiting at a crossroads
    calls him by this name. He hears from the bill of the bird
which way he must go, and he knows that the seer
    before him is blind, its eyes sealed tight
    in a specimen of sleep. A blind bird there
at the bottom of the ocean. Nanasimgit,
    as if reaching for some secret feature of his body,
    as if reaching for a thought that is sheathed in his brain,
draws the knife that rests in its place at his side,
    the knife he has crafted in patient days,
    in stroke after stroke at the honing stone.
He takes that blade where his mind meets
    the world, and he cradles the head of the bird in his hand,
    the softness of feathers like a child's hair in his palm.
And with all the skill of breathing underwater
    he touches his knife to where the eyelids meet,
    and here, a mere film from the delicate eye,

he makes an incision that matches its curve,
    slits and slips the two eyelids apart.
    He does this right and he does this left,
opens the eye-crack that opens the light,
    opens the smooth swaying green of the waters.
    He watches world granted where there was no world,
and from the goose comes the undammed pouring of thanks,
    the praise of the gorgeous in the praise of its eyes.
    And Nanasimgit is blessed by what his blade has healed.

## 8. The Fire God Is Found in Wood

Agni, the god of fire, is exhausted—
    needs to flee to where no devotee can find him.
    Agni, who'd lift his rippling fingers
in praise of other gods, transmuting every sacrifice
    to smoke and scent, needs a reprieve
    from the relentlessly pious. He hides—who would look
for him there?—in water. He enters a pool
    with hissing and bubbling, lounges there
    for hours unaddressed—until he is outed
by an indignant, sweltering frog.
    Agni still needs to conceal himself,
    hides in the ringed and fibrous cool of trees.
It is not long before rumors find him. Like
    any god he is half-willing to be found. Wood
    is broken open to reveal the fleeting
figure of the god, his quick body writhing
    in the case of its hive, the voice of his godhead
    running liquid with flame, with a litheness
that purifies all it erases. Agni flees
    impish from the cool compact wood,
    a flourish of tattered orange light and revelation.
Near-humans became the guardians of fire.
    They'd seen lightning strike in white jags to Earth,
    watched it fracturing, severing the sky,
seen its fire savage through a stand of trees.
    They found the god hidden in the core of wood,
    and this heavenly body was granted to their keeping.
They learned to hold it rapacious in their hands:
    there in their center a small tamed star,
    a magic all contortion and flickering of flame.
They compassed themselves to a perfect circle,
    each one of their faces a point on its wheel.
    They were lit by this newly captive light.
It was the badge that marked them from the animals.
    It was the gift and theft and treasure of the gods.
    They were the blazing mages of the world,

and this new magic licked at their brains.
   They had plucked the blossoms of the stars,
   and the features of their faces would never be still.

**9. Israelites and Others Travel to a Promise**

The ancestors spread from one blessed valley
    to cover the world, a human film
    stretching over a planet peopled by animals.
The Israelites escape from generations' captivity,
    stagger through a desert that will barely support them,
    trudging the dead zone between memory and future.
They bang against the borders of their maps,
    follow the image of the shifting phantasmal:
    chasing cloud and following fire.
The Israelites are somewhere in a voyage of magic
    where water gushes live from rock,
    bread drops in bakers' flakes from the sky.
They hope for a land that will spread itself out
    munificent before them, a parcel of the Earth
    to claim as their own. In exhaustion they hurl
themselves forward, dreaming each night
    of warm milk, herbaceous honey,
    tasting this sweetness on the grit of their tongues.
The ancestors, arriving, were dumber than the animals:
    reckless, destructive, understanding nothing.
    They read the newly opened text of a region,
deciphered the ground and the fauna around them,
    acquired the lore of leaf and root,
    found their minds freshly tooled to its newness.
They made each grace or inhospitality home,
    began to dream the landscape where they lived,
    molded stories of who they would be in this place.

## 10. Seven Brothers Make a Team

When their journey begins they cannot be distinguished:
    seven brothers, numbered and unnamed,
    blank ordinals of family. They arrive
at the crossroads where the story divides them;
    and when they meet here again at the end of a year
    each has been blessed with a gift, a trick
to untie a particular knot in their plot.
    Magic spectacles allow one to see
    each feather on a bird a hundred miles away.
The flying carpet rolled under his arm lets another
    transport them in a blink to remotest lands.
    A violin reduces to slumber a whole, now snoring
contingent of soldiers. An unexceptional-looking coat
    has capacious pockets, could conceal an elephant.
    A twig that waved lightly blossoms to cudgels
that chase and bruise their enemies maroon.
    A bow to shoot an arrow to the eye
    of that hundred-mile bird. An arm now blessed
with the strength to catch, ease down, whatever falls,
    no matter its weight, sand grain to millstone.
    They are men of miracle, figures of fantasy,
and the gathering of their talents anticipates their story.
    They form a nexus of separate selves,
    dexterous and complex as the digits of a hand.
Now they are characters who can animate a tale,
    rescue a princess, foil a magician,
    wrap the world around their clever little fingers.
And now these somewhat human beings,
    stirring with a Vishnu-seed inside them,
    entered this mutual magic of inflation.
They pressed their way from pack to team,
    formed themselves to an aggregate being,
    took contiguous roles, practiced actions,
parsed tasks to rough component parts,
    laid plans on a mental map of the land:
    granular creatures now smoothed and sheeted,

defeating together what surpassed them in might.
> A triumph of thread was pulled taut through their brains,
> the nerves of one system stretching between them.

They were a galvanized, storied assemblage
> powerful enough to drag mammoths to ground,
> inhabit an imagined and multiplied scale.

They had become a creature of legend,
> an ordonnance of muscle and tendriling thought,
> a complex formidable multi-limbed beast.

## 11. Speech Ignites Muhammad's Mouth

The larynx lowered for formation of sounds;
    our progenitors babbled to find phonemic range.
    And in the miracling of words from rudimentary soundings
new clothes were cut to fit their lives,
    a magic of air was matched to thing,
    each object called by its spirit, its name.
Muhammad—and may peace be upon him and upon
    each flowering of his speech—is wombed in stone,
    listening and waiting for his story to begin—
sitting in that clarified attention of prayer.
    There flashes the forked lightning-strike of speech;
    the skies pour themselves to channels of words
as each night of silence blossoms within him.
    And the angel of the tongue of God—
    this tongue that has been courting him all his life—
resounds in the charge of the molecules around him,
    in all the tunnels and mansions of his ears—
    breaks open its singular imperative: *speak:*
whether or not you're a man of letters,
    whether you are gifted with the luster of language,
    whether you know where words' hearts might incline.
Our forebears lit on the sound of each visible thing,
    rewaking the world in the motion of their mouths;
    granting each animal its shape on their tongues,
inventing new water, new stone, new falling and splash.
    They named the sun, the rain, the powers of the skies.
    They donned the deep blue jacket of thought.
They were entranced by the cadences of speech,
    the intimate communion of mouth and ear,
    this lovely susurrus of wonder among them.
Muhammad is called to angelic vocation,
    to stand to other listeners as the angel stands to him:
    to be font and vessel and bestower of speech,
the voice that peels open heaven's revelations.
    He hears a single verse, then another,
    is pregnant with all the verses to come.

People picked the air with imagination's knife;
    words reached beyond the life they knew,
    gleamed with the shine of fat on their lips.
They were given the grace of storied minds,
    their love of existence was lifted in language,
    and the wondrous wreaked its desires on their lives.
They set to dancing in the mirrors of themselves,
    voyaged and bled in others' skin,
    heard rumblings within the bowels of the land,
invitations spoken by animal and sky,
    and the universe was met as a vastness with a voice,
    in hymns unearthed in the shadow of their tongues.
Muhammad's lithe body of listening is worked
    like lace, calligraphy adorning the windows
    and doorways of his mind. He's the site where speech
sets foot upon Earth. Language reverberates
    on every audible horizon, and in every
    direction he turns is the cascading angel.

## 12. David and the Soothing of Music

They were blessed with new voices to sing of the world,
    pitches that placed them within the order of creation,
    granted them clean access to exquisite making.
They knew in their throats the human thirst for beauty,
    knew it too in the music that issued from their hands
    as drums elaborated their own tripping hearts,
bones shaped and warmed the tones of breath,
    and tune was composed from the tautness of strings.
    Music matched and mapped the freshly human soul,
swelled in sorrow and joy and the shadings where they met,
    in ease and some newly limitless longing
    that bound them to the birds and the soaring spheres.
A boy shepherd wanders humming in the hills,
    a youth whose lithe body is supple as a lyre,
    whose music is renowned as a medicine of spirit.
He's enlisted to soothe the bristles of the king,
    ease and disarm Saul's implacable demons.
    David plucks gut to ordered emotions,
his fingers drawing misery and its matched consolation,
    charting the intervals of the disconsolate soul,
    the temporal circuit from grief to its completion.
Music softened the darkness, scattered it with stars,
    distilled balm from the deepest malaise of a life,
    cracked open the rich proffered hive of the sublime.
A luminous clothing is laid on the world,
    a graciousness enhancing the scope of the human,
    and David's are the fingers by which it arrives.

## 13. Jesus Is Rebuked, Art Takes Flight

From the impressionable mud by the river
    the idle boy-Jesus shapes figures of sparrows
    with the care, the absorption of a child at play.
The rabbis do not like what they see,
    accuse him of the vicious blasphemy of image.
    Jesus, disrupted, disturbed, indignant,
flails his arms and shouts the whole flock
    of them up into flight—the birds now utterly
    beyond him: what was mere graven mud
now alert and sentient, translated to life.
    Jesus watches the scattering of sparrows
    to the broad, unparented air, gazes up
to the light from beneath their quick shadows,
    delights in their swift unpredictable fleeting,
    knows what he has created cannot be wrong.
People crept into caves with pots of pigment,
    apprehended in the dark the figures of animals,
    pressed their minds upon the unpainted world.
Animals in majesty stepped into stone,
    were doubled as creatures, translated to image,
    rock now sleighted to a testament of wonder.
Bison wandered heavily up from dreams,
    reindeer caught in their antlers the signals
    of the sky, and horses, breathing unutterable
peace, were held in human reverence.
    Still we taste their discovery on our tongues,
    know these makers of image share blood with us.
They pressed through the visible to invisible lives,
    calling the luminous to the surface of stone,
    and striding more deeply through waking and dream.

## 14. Praise

Praise the drifting through the silent halls of creation,
that spinning inside one old couple's bodies
were hidden such starlight, such flurry of forms.

Praise the protean profusion of mammals,
the twisting to multiply marvelous forms,
the exultation in fur and cunning and speed.

Praise that sport of flight and plumage,
of melody lifted from caverns of bereavement.
Praise the flair and excess in the signature of being,

the plenitude, profusion, that pours from its lips,
the craving for uncountable variations of life.
Praise the persistent revision of the hominid

form, the makers' patient return to their craft;
the body's sensorium, its palette of pleasures,
its every physical prerequisite of mind.

And the slicing open of bright prophetic eyes,
the tools that sharpen and reorder the world;
the capture of landed god, earthed magic,

the cradling of fire in bold humanoid hands;
the spreading of forebears through the habitable world,
every strange and discoverable land of promise;

the brothers who enhance and arrange themselves to story,
teaming to tackle insuperable prey.
Praise the genesis and genius of language,

the cataract Muhammad's mouth has become,
the radiation of speech beyond the material,
the swelling evocation of invisible worlds.

Praise music written on matter's own bones,
the consolation that quiets the nerves of a king;
the hands that make art and know this worship,

that release it to arc and wing on the air.
Praise the sacred human commission of making,
the wonder of the world newly shining in our eyes.

*Five*

## 1. Listening

Humans were alert with a further listening,
the wavering of air before a surge of change.

They listened, hungry, for a new food to feed them,
a plump and elaborate new order of lives.

They listened to land and for a story that sought them,
for a device that would plant them further in place

and recast the nature of what they were.
They listened for faint wishes to germinate

inside them, listened darkly at the cuspids
of thought, strained to hear a narrative floating

toward them, glimpse the outlines of nascent gods
hiding and stalking in dapplings of flora.

They listened with fingers, appetites, eyes,
with the heritable thirst for what has not been.

They probed for the moment of the next press forward,
for the malleable where the human might again be modeled.

## 2. Seeds Are Sown, Plants Spring Up

A card is flipped; there steps out, grinning,
    the harlequin sower, scattering his lavish fine
    seed to soil, that he might engorge
the moist and fecund belly of the Earth.
    He scatters madly on stones and thorns,
    on the path where seeds will be crushed to death.
The sower casts unstintingly into mute future—
    in the folly of tossing stored treasure to wind—
    dispensing the cherished like a dusting of stars.
Roamers who had lived as wild in the world
    acquired the slow-motion magic of seeds,
    found life in the tiny packed kernels of death,
threw what was most precious onto the dirt,
    transforming precious nothings to baskets that brimmed,
    moving with the liturgy of land and its seasons.
They ventured to magnify natural abundance:
    sacrifice grains and wait for them to bear;
    turn green that was given to a green of their own.
Seasonal villages rooted to permanence,
    numbers swelled with serial births, and farmers
    were blessed with an excess to store and defend.
With bread they were sifted into strata,
    some fraction of their hands now freed from labor,
    those who toiled now shouldering more.
The sower scatters seeds as if he were blind,
    dispatches them with his time-crazed words:
    Die, be as grain, and you'll be born.
He keeps stepping back to the dark of the grave,
    wandering inside that womb of abundance,
    and painting fresh faces on the rising grain.

## 3. Circe Domesticates Animal-Men

Animals were enclosed within the fence
    of human wills, the most trusting species
    tamed to yield meat and milk, acquiring
a docility at human hands and turning
    from wild to domesticated bodies. People
    made themselves lords of their animal underlings,
turned sheep and goats and cows to chattel,
    the neotenic nurtured and led to their slaughter.
    They sheltered birds to feed on their eggs;
crafted biddable species from the bodies of wolves,
    mounted themselves on magnificent steeds,
    brought the wild world within their orders.
One morning's reconnaissance and Odysseus's men
    are robbed of their beloved bodies, winked
    into creatures bewildering to themselves:
from men of dignity and civilized pride
    to these trundling sacs of grunt and hunger,
    snouts rooting at the slurry of their forfeited lives.
Stunned by this necromantic transformation,
    they are flesh to flesh with naked comrades,
    their sleek warrior bodies gorged and swollen,
swarming in the singular urgency of need—
    truncheoned by compulsions that eclipse all their thought,
    magicked from honor to the riot of the pig pen.
They carry some ghost of their former lives,
    some elusive memory of their finer selves,
    are tantalized, taunted, by what they were.
Minor characters now within Circe's drama,
    ferried like children through the unhoured days,
    they owe her their purest religious fear.
They fatten themselves toward coming carnage.
    An enchantress has intervened between them and their lives
    and they croon to her as svelte suitors to the moon.

## 4. Ganesha Splits Himself, Writing Appears

Ganesha, that fubsy elephant-boy of a god,
    hears the electric Mahabharata, is galvanized
    by these lines that must not disappear,
that must be set down in each cadence and phrase,
    in every unparaphrased, unsummarized word.
    He is marooned without stylus or pen
as the words flow over his rippling ears.
    He would offer any limb of his body for their sake:
    between himself and the story there is no choosing.
Ganesha knows himself servant of these lines
    that dream his life; he will inscribe their holiness
    at whatever severing cost to himself.
His human hands grip his elephant's tusk, wrenching
    his body away from itself, torquing to meet
    that sharp report, that snapping of his wholeness.
Ganesha, broken into body and pen,
    holds his own amputated tusk in his hand;
    is the zealous amanuensis of the purling epic.
He soaks the sharp point of himself in ink,
    watches in wonder the wet black of its tip,
    the darkness that sings like speech on page.
He feels the smooth cool weight of ivory,
    its perfect ease as it glides on white,
    the way it warms in his scribing hand.
We first learned to set numbers, accounts;
    learned to layer symbols on the symbols
    of speech, to impress our words upon the world,
inscribing designs of lapidary beauty,
    geometries of thought, bright alphabetic bits:
    placing these firmly in the order of matter.
With writing arose a refinement of mind,
    a recalling of the articulate and propelling it forward
    in the setting and mending and revising of lines.
Holiness was encoded in repetitions of speech;
    the voices of others spoke in absentia,
    granting them the status of gods and ghosts.

Words transcended, surprised their speakers;
    a descending tongue reshaped the reader's mouth.
    We were entranced by flexuous texts,
the streaming evolution of lexical complexity,
    the intricate spangled jewelry-work of lines;
    were forever embellished, overlaced with words.

**5. Religions Arrive with the Gifts of the Fairies**

When for the christening of the augured princess
    twelve golden plates are laid on the table
    and invitations dispatched to the kingdom's wise women,
they converge from all the points of the hours,
    sweep in to the palace in their rainbow of hues,
    their gowns trailing broken tokens of Earth.
As they encircle this infant, this cynosure,
    the surrounding court stills itself to listen,
    to watch as benison descends before their eyes.
The fairy women pour out the golden bowls
    of their offerings, murmur their music as they ring
    the girl, bestowing the generous spectrum of goodness.
They plant the child richly with seminal virtues,
    clothe her in the pristine linen of future.
    They gift her with charisms: with beauty, with vision,
with kindness of heart, a curious mind,
    with knowledge and its guiding wisdom,
    with the patience of hope and ease of peace.
They grant her grace of speech, a measured
    humility, and that stirring urge to creation.
    What is spoken dusts the child,
a treasury of charms infuses her skin,
    and the tints beneath her eyelids shift
    in this great emollient laying on of light.
Eleven fairies have uttered a near-
    perfect blessing; only one of their number
    remains to speak—and there's a ruckus at the door.
People discovered an inscription within the sleeve
    of their lives, a radiance that shone in the world
    about them; they struck against the jewels in their days;
cherished these, fingered them, crafted them into
    ritual and prayer. They lit on phrases,
    on motions that opened pathways of the holy;
and the muzzle of the numinous grazed their days.
    They discovered the world as a theatre of worship,
    attended on the sacred in the grottoes of their flesh.

A man sits stilled in the moonlit shade of a tree
    until a universe blossoms within him
    and he is the mirror where creation is displayed.
Visited men become tongues of God,
    become, reluctantly, figures of fire
    carrying covenant, imperative, praise.
There sashays the princely paragon, exciter of our love,
    the blue-skinned enticer seducing with his flute.
    Women craft the wondrous stories of the world,
hearing and honing tales that slide
    with the colors and sure liquidity of dream,
    with all the topoi of the divine in the days.
A man is told as a visit of God,
    the munificent pouring of love and forgiveness,
    the extravagant washing of the world in perfume.
An ascetic sits in patience in a cave
    until everything incarnates itself in his language,
    calling to a singleness all the motes of the world.
The holy appears in its plethora of forms;
    each religion pours the gorgeous of its own.
    It is good—and there's a ruckus at the door.

## 6. Muhammad Meets the Foreign

Nubs of people discovered each other,
    traversing the distances that had held them distinct,
    dispersed human dust now craving coalescence.
They peered across the swinging rope-bridge of culture,
    cast glances over the high fences of themselves,
    coveted foreign secrets and skills, tools
and talents granted to alien hands, their ingenious
    molding of the substances of Earth. Curious, they
    listened with some fields of themselves in suspension,
as what had been unimaginable found its face.
    They warred and hated; they traded: the unfamiliar
    refused, desired, resisted, absorbed.
A winged horse flashes gold against the black
    of the sky, glistens with the lizard, the dragon,
    the stallion's sweat, travels at a story's
equivalent of the speed of light. The princely
    rider, the mouth of God, is soaring
    on the draft of wild inspiration, through
the cleansing and rippling high cold on his skin.
    Muhammad is winging his way to Jerusalem
    on this silken fantastic magic carpet;
summoned, trusting, to this meeting his mind
    cannot conceive. He alights on a hilltop,
    faces the venerable, the patriarchs, the prophets,
dismounts to pray with Abraham, Moses, and Jesus,
    with the line of his predecessors as voices of the holy;
    and the hands of their hearts are linked in circuit.
They stand in a circle with foreign lands and times,
    with the voices of other scripts and texts,
    to forge a ring of the corners of the world.
Regions learned to converse with each other
    at the swarming caravanserais of human encounter.
    They lived beside strangers until they were unstrange,
savored delectable flavors new to their mouths,
    grafted new holinesses onto what they'd known,
    learned to wander across the borders of stories.

They met as on a mountain where they could survey
    all the rich and valleyed kingdoms
    and breed what isolation could not have conceived.
Muhammad is a needle stitching heavens to Earth,
    knows the sacred as a blending of long-aligned musics,
    a fecundity leaved with silver and gold.
He stands as any man upon Earth,
    knows that words like wells are hidden everywhere
    and water, sweet, is nowhere to be scorned.

## 7. Odysseus and the Underworld

Odysseus cannot evade the summons,
    the voyage that plunges him beneath his human life
    down to the wonderrealm of shades. There is
no way home but this absolute fall: succumbing
    to where gravity can lure him no lower. He breaches
    the portentous threshold of the worlds, moves
as grumous flesh through a viscosity of shadows.
    He submits to the fertile black, enacts
    the ritual list of demands, slices open the throats
of oxen, pours blood, keeps pouring blood. The blood
    runs till it overflows the trough, runs
    till there is nothing in the world but blood.
There are voices at every point on the circle
    of his sight, voices which will not settle
    to selves. Progenitors and prophets swarm
around him with all the anonymous infectious dead.
    Odysseus pivots with his red sword before him,
    invites each shade singly to drink and speak,
hears words that strike as pick to rock.
    His future streams cleanly from Tiresias's tongue
    in the speech he is given to tint all his days.
Odysseus is dipped, by Tiresias's words,
    by each succeeding scene in Hades,
    in blackness so saturate it bends toward light.
He hefts the weight of his obsidian fortune,
    this gift he has schemed to coax the world forward.
    He meets his own part in this unfurling epic,
and an ichoring sweetness engorges his veins.
    Humanity could not refrain from making,
    human tissue the new salt sea of creation.
We continued to heal the grievous gap
    between our lives and the beauty of the sacred.
    We became miners for compacted light;
lingered in the antechambers of dreams, rummaged
    in the endless dress-up chests of the cosmos.
    Intuitions poked through the borders of the known;

we pursued the body's still perilous anacondas
    of light, sought further stars within the skull. Our
    mouths could now birth such arias of brilliance, elicit
elation, rinse the great thirsting human
    sensorium, and buoy us for moments beyond the borders
    of our skin. In the theatre where each needle of genius
is threaded, we found beauty that would flense the skin
    from our flesh, glimpsed some ecstatic version
    of ourselves, that play of surface with pellucid
depth, the tossing of world through its mirror
    and back. We dove and dared to enter
    the realm where all marvel is kept for safekeeping.

## 8. Story and Dream

The making itself, this rapturous procession,
might be in its nature both event and telling:
all physics and chemistry, biology and history
blessed with the arc and cadence of story—
a sequence of scenes that reveals us as we read.
Dream suffuses the fabric of this world,

shines on the life we wake to and from.
We wade through the living streams beneath us,
relent to become the lives we are not, dissolve
to the wider world and its walking. We wake
from story to story, dream into dream,
the Scheherazade layers with which we are stained.

Creatures of fancy as much as of flesh,
we live in bestowal of image, incantation of line.
We shift with the fictions at the core of the cosmos,
the deep draw of matter toward metamorphosis, are held
in this intimate mingling of sublime and solid,
this lineage of vision that gives rise to our lives,

the dreamdark that emerges as song from our mouths.
The holy is our immersion, drowning in story,
a gold chain that cinches our moments to devotion,
a conspiracy of lushness, ebullience, beauty.
We live in the poetry connate in the cosmos,
the stories that rise from the roots of matter,

the dreams that keep streaming toward what might be.
Mystery keeps liberating itself from the given,
and our blessing is this laying our lives upon story,
witnessing as the world is zipped together
in this telling that wants itself, telling and charm.
We know that story-words speak the world whole,

shuck and shine the dailiness they're given,
free us and stretch us taut in time,
fill and fit and repeal our silence.
There are rivers stroked by princes that purl
beneath our sleep, stories that keep calling
for our lives to fill their banks. And born

with such longing for narrative élan, for scene
that flows from vivid scene, for euphony
and the delicate jewelry of words, we are restless
until we come to ourselves in story, until
we know ourselves bright with dream,
until welcomed, embraced, by the myths of our making.

## 9. Draupadi and the World, Stripped and Unstrippable

A clutch of men is attempting to view
    this magnificent woman who has, at their bidding,
    entered the room. They're intent on peeling
what keeps her curved body from their sight; and Draupadi,
    in her wish to remain unshamed before them,
    composes herself in prayer to Lord Krishna:
that he might protect her from the lust of their eyes.
    She is stilled with Krishna in unmoving meditation;
    in her mind one note is rung and resounds.
The men are curious, covetous, appraise her,
    this prize they have recently won at dice.
    They anticipate their eyes as hands roaming freely
over this supple flesh that is theirs.
    They grasp one end of her sari, pull
    to remove the fine covering from the world.
It pours from her body like oracle, spring;
    folds and folds are gathered in their hands—
    a vast wealth of fabric, a fortune of silk,
bolt upon bolt rucked and lapping on the floor—
    the wardrobe of thousands spun from one woman.
    The minds of the men are stretched to bursting.
She revolves in the spectacular magic of her god:
    a top that tantalizes their every desire,
    a marvel of molting who will never be nude.
The curious among humans listened to the languages
    of animal, plant, and star, the at-first
    indecipherable tongues of flesh and stone,
listened to the inscrutable minutiae of Earth.
    They aspired to a clean unmediated knowledge,
    something their senses could seal as true.
They craved a place where people spoke only
    the raw unclothed order of the given world.
    They decrypted the holiness laid down in matter,
found patterns pulsing within the spheres' old music—
    another symphonic system of knowledge.
    The human eye transcended its scale,

glassed itself to peer to vast and tiny worlds,
    sliced into the mystery of the human body.
    They began to solve the riddles which the universe spoke,
dissected to minuter particles and forces
    the hymns and holy texts of the cosmos,
    unearthing a wondrously granular revelation,
a precocious younger sibling. The world shifted its weight
    to its other foot, disclosed a further ark of laws,
    loosing fixed stars and completed revelation.
We were blessed as tinkers and tasters of the cosmos;
    the world was illumined by this mining of light
    as human life adjusted the angle of its axis.
And for all we discovered the world was still composed:
    Draupadi still spinning, that dervish of undress;
    the drapery of this Earth not yet exhausted.

## 10. Praise

Praise the seeds that pool in human hands,
that are scattered freely, in prodigal sweep,
the tilling of ground for all that will follow.

Praise the placid tractable animals
herded into some queer human household,
for Circe's witchery, transformation of flesh.

Praise the revision of body, of tusk and eye,
to record and read stories that steam from the mind,
the transmutation of darkness into legible script.

Praise the gifts of magnanimous bestowing fairies,
the figures who formulate the holy of the world,
the wealth of scripture, ritual, wisdom.

And the flight of a winged bedizened horse,
the linking of unthinkable corners of the Earth,
the weaving of tongues and prayers on a mountaintop.

Praise the pouring of bull blood black into trench,
the ringing voice of the prophetic that echoes in our skulls,
the cauled and interred we lift into light.

Praise this world that births us, creatures emergent
from dream and from story—these rivers of image
that clothe and entice us with brightness. Praise

the blazing white light of invention,
the body of darkness craving tongue,
the candescent slow-motion seedburst of creation;

the dance of a veiled and available cosmos,
the bolts of knowledge that flow through our hands,
this beauty we never strip to its skin.

*Six*

## 1. Listening

We listened with hope and a softness of caution
to the knowledge that fluttered at the edges of our senses,

the marvels that might yet be granted to our hands.
We listened as a safecracker for the world to release,

for the flicking of a page beyond our known world;
a tickle of brilliance there within our skulls.

The long-abraded planet listened with us,
listened as from the hazy, troubled verges of sleep:

shifting and waiting for the next note to fall.
We listened for something at once acceleration,

revelation; the track of racing human momentum—
for what of the unmade we could yet lure to be.

## 2. Adam and Eve and the Arrival of Industry

Then the sudden galvanizing power of steam,
    a fierce solar fuel locked deep in the Earth,
    dark material yielding near-infinite energy.
Here was magic enacted under cover of smoke,
    a rupture in the forces acting on the land.
    Here also a scene of unblemished innocence.
Here are our handsome unblushing progenitors
    gliding through the dew of the cool morning garden,
    standing in the pretty dappled shade of the forbidden.
They are, in their every fresh cell, blessed with hunger,
    blessed with precious newborn curiosity.
    The tree stretches up like a ladder to the sky,
to that great wide world where creators must live;
    and they long to peer out with the wide eyes of gods,
    hoisted above the ground where they stand.
They're gripped by the great human lust for advancement—
    that imagined bounty rippling at the curtains
    of all they can conceive. They steal within a world
still satin, unweighted by consequence, a time
    unsullied by history, and the luscious fruit tantalizes:
    longs, they are certain, to taste their lips.
Machinery, that bracing revelation, granted us
    the status of mages, compressed in a jar
    the force of scores of workers. It produced a dizzying
profusion of goods, blistered the world
    with bargains, an ersatz new face of nature,
    a brazen second order of human making.
Fingers jointly close about that globe of flesh
    in the fervent, forgivable grasp of desire,
    the wish for the dominion and indulgence of gods.
They pluck, they scent the fruit in their hands,
    brush it against the anticipation of their lips,
    test it and take it with the need of their teeth—
relish it on every uncharted corner of their tongues.
    It is, as promised, delicious, divine.
    They wonder only why they waited so long.

And we, triumphant makers, radiant consumers,
    were entranced by pleasure, purchased and plucked,
    immersed in a world that spread itself for us.
Purring convenience crept into our lives,
    granted us unprecedented ease,
    permitted us to be more elaborately human.
A corollary blackness stained the sky;
    sludge poured unctuous to river and soil;
    toxins seeped to the homes and warrens of the world.
Granted entry to the tightly guarded palace of the gods,
    they eat themselves into a gluttony of hunger,
    find their bodies now impervious to full.
Their fingers let the cores drop beneath laden boughs,
    obedience, caducous, tossed with the pits.
    They conspire to plant whole orchards of this tree,
to uproot each unnecessary unprofitable plant,
    modernize this garden into plantation.
    The world was so clothed in novel manufacture
our eyes could find nowhere not humanly made.
    Land was lost to our intimate wonder,
    the heaven of invisibles lifted from our lives.
And if there's an angel, cicerone of their future,
    who guides a tour of the centuries to come,
    they see that their transgression bears also good fortune.
They have wreaked untellable affliction on the planet;
    the world is in ruins and could not have advanced
    without this precise verboten act.

## 3. Raven Is Reassembled with the City and the Nation

Raven's body has been hacked to fragments:
    bones shattered, flesh mashed to pulp,
    toes contorted, beak a broken compass,
feathers a matting of shattered twigs,
    tendons and muscles a tangle of the useless.
    The scraps of him molder in the world's latrine.
He could give himself up for garbage,
    suffocate beneath the incessant defecation.
    Or assemble himself from slop and shards.
Raven can barely remember the fiction
    of himself. Exhausted, weary beyond weariness,
    he tugs on frayed threads to pull himself together,
intuits some draw of him to him, drags
    parts though there is no *he* to do anything.
    He stitches someone from dull lumps
of viscera, some seamed and cicatriced simulacrum
    of himself. He puppeteers his piecemeal body.
    Nothing quite precisely fits:
a misshapen model of what bird might be;
    an advent of something jerried, kludged—
    an Easter morning all covered with shit.
People were drawn by gravity to cities,
    abandoned old fields for the swollen metropolitan,
    detached from the cycles of discarded nature.
They amassed to broader aggregate bodies,
    leapt onto each other to form human pyramids,
    dared themselves to figures of stability and strength.
They were thrilled by a bracing urban speed,
    a jolting caffeine of pace and urgency;
    met fierce anonymity, the unsewered, diseased.
Forests were felled for urban grain,
    fields further enlarged to claim animal habitat,
    land learning human, losing animal tongues.
Raven grins as his own lopsided invention:
    the raucous, illicit, grossly indecent,
    the lacquering of blackness over open wound.

He's the nearly convincing forgery of himself:
>   a splintered, duct-taped flock, an unkindness,
>   a conspiracy of all the trash he's made of.
The complex eusocial ant palace cities
>   burgeoned to vast and buzzing masses.
>   Residents imagined themselves members of nations,
conceived themselves as conglomerate giants,
>   creatures rising from slumber beneath mountains and hills,
>   great folkloric beings who lumbered through the world.
They sliced the planet into tranches of identity,
>   erased their differences with nearer neighbors,
>   defined themselves against some more distant foreign.
And everything that was not them was exploitable.
>   Tied by strings to the head of their cities,
>   they were the urban, the national, were us.

## 4. Jacob and Nations Steal a Blessing

Nations planted flags on distant soil,
    extracted riches from foreign lands:
    gold and silver, fur and timber,
rubber and tea, chocolate and coffee,
    the dark drinking pleasures of the one pale world.
    Whole continents were taken, enlisted as suppliers.
Contact arrived with decimating death:
    poxes that assisted intended genocide,
    the deliberate efficient clear-cutting of natives.
The world was sorted to servant and served,
    bodies caged and auctioned to buyers,
    tradition and religion stamped into soil,
everything indigenous defined as pernicious;
    unfathomed artworks marveled at, considered,
    lifted to grace imperial museums.
Children were abducted, converted to strange cultures,
    weeping for absent families as they sat at their desks,
    ancient languages scrubbed from their tongues.
The aging patriarch is to pass on his blessing:
    good fortune can fall only one of two ways.
    Isaac instructs his firstborn to prepare him a meal:
venison from the field, sauced the way he likes.
    Esau with his bow exeunts from his father
    while outside the tent his mother crouches, all ears.
She prefers the younger, smooth-skinned Jacob,
    spreads before him her hoodwinking plan.
    Rebecca can manipulate the future from the kitchen,
spice a kid so it's as gamy as venison,
    deceive the most vivid of her husband's senses.
    Isaac's eyes are glaucous, dim;
a bit of vocal coaching, amateur theatre,
    and their futures are fixed. On Jacob's neck
    and forearms she straps goatskins that mimic
Esau's fur, plucks her eldest's second set of clothes.
    Jacob in pantomime stands in costume with gift,
    having practiced his lines, his testosteroned voice.

Jacob names himself Esau, proffers food
> in exchange for a tumbling lineage of wealth.
> But Isaac has suspicious ears,
detects a voice not quite right in timbre;
> his fingers braille the hairy arms;
> he sniffs the sharpness of Esau's animal sweat.
Isaac's nostrils are soothed by hunting and blood;
> he's restless to be relieved of his gift,
> to be generous to the one who pleasures his palate.
Isaac pours out his unstinting blessing,
> rains upon Jacob all the fat of the Earth:
> abundance of food and dark flowing wine
for him and his infinite line of descendants.
> Their bodies will be nourished, their tastes indulged,
> they'll eat when all around them starve.
He'll be lord over his brother Jacob,
> and all other nations will bow before him;
> the dew of heaven will be his.
Every cell in Jacob's body
> feels itself thicken with globules of fat.
> When Esau makes his entry with the savory game,
he takes in, in one glance, the thespian costume
> and props, the pathetic mechanics of theft,
> is desperate to recover what he has lost.
Old Isaac admits that he's been duped,
> that he and the future have been victims of trickery.
> The purse of a blind man's words has been stolen.
Esau rails at his unmoving father:
> Could you not discern your firstborn from a goat?
> Will you not restore what you know has been stolen?
Isaac has held in his mouth no more than one blessing,
> cannot redirect his misspoken words,
> grants to Esau only generations of abasement.

## 5. Raven and We Find a Double Face

Raven stands on the snowball he has formed,
    the poised and balanced ball of Earth.
    And there's an itch that instigates somewhere
beneath his beak, an itch that has never
    troubled him before. Using his wing
    like the thumb side of a hand, he pushes
up against his great beak, his bird face
    slides up to the crown of his head, his
    great cape of feathers slips back from his shoulders
and descends from his body like necessary tears.
    Beneath that old sly and corvid face,
    hidden like a star within a dark box,
the soft nose, whited eyes, the fleshy lips,
    the unanticipated angles of cheek and chin.
    He finds the face beneath his face,
these long and narrow limbs, and he
    locates himself in this story's beguilement.
    What are his lips begin by grinning.
Scientists cracked open the carapace of history,
    lighting the chambers of the once before our time;
    they learned to listen to the language of stone,
came to tell time in the strata of rock.
    They read runic lines the planet had laid down;
    geology divulged a new revelation,
opened curtains on a time where a story could be told.
    Humans stumbled, curious, on fossils and conundrums,
    watched animals twisting, miraculous, Ovidian,
into the wondrous forms of themselves;
    they glimpsed the first lacunaed albums
    of our familial life, watched the process in precision
move before their eyes: finches and beetles
    and butterflies becoming; found themselves in an unfinished
    scripture, the forest and pool of metamorphosis.
They gazed across the threshold of myth-worlds and world,
    projected, in crude brief clips, the grainy
    halting film of creation. They had lit

upon the hidden workshop where making occurs,
>   the unhumanly patient practice of revision,
>   were vacant of myth that could cast these to sense.
They interpreted the antiquated dialects of the dead
>   as their forebears swarmed and multiplied before them;
>   and they found there is no fish or insect,
no reptile or raptor, no green sprouting plant,
>   no scurrying rodent or crouching simian,
>   no breath of being unconnected to us.
They discovered that we are autochthonous creatures,
>   not distinct from the one long arc of song.
>   They were blessed and bewildered and bereft.
Raven peers out at all the whiteness of the world,
>   is forever doubled, the other of himself.
>   He cannot slam shut the new doors of his face.
He is the newly opened residence
>   of old and nested and shifting forms,
>   the wiliness of crossing the blade of the worlds.

## 6. The Heavens Address Us and Put Us in Our Place

When Rama has slipped beneath the surface of himself,
    made concessions unworthy of a less noble man;
    when he has died to his love for Sita,
would send the one he's worshiped to the fire of exile;
    when Rama has become a stranger to Rama,
    an amnesia of the redeemer he was born to be—
the sky splits open to accost, correct him.
    There descends an armada of all the great gods,
    chariots crowded with the features and the multiple
limbs of divinity: Brahma and Shiva,
    Indra and Agni, Lakshmi, Durga
    and Sarasvati, the myriad variations
of those who are cosmos, are goddess and god.
    Rama's own purest shape rides with them,
    the doubleness of his own alpha and omega,
the Vishnu of all he originally, ultimately is;
    and Rama, depleted of quiddity, faces
    himself, his essence, core of his cores.
The gods lean as orators over the chassis
    of their celestial cars, address the muddled one
    who is their font, proclaim to Rama who he is,
lavishing their words on his parched human skin,
    calling him by his human and heavenly names:
    You are Rama, you are Vishnu,
the single source of the black coiling making,
    the cool blue of wonder at the waking of worlds,
    the dreamer whose breath is the spring of all being,
the one unfurling incense and music of creation.
    Yours is the body that gives birth to all beauty,
    the holy syllable sounding from the stars.
The gods peel back his memory
    to the eons before his Earthly birth,
    restore him to his sleek encompassing history,
recite to him the sweep of his coruscating epic
    as the daring blue avatar of descent and redemption.
    They rechristen him in his original name,

cradle him within the vast tale he has been;
    speak him that he might inhabit himself,
    move as Vishnu in this current of world.
We unraveled the lineage laid down in our flesh,
    the origin and long ramification of life;
    narrated the intricate organism Earth,
the formation of circling planets and sun.
    We charted the elaborate genealogy of stars,
    traced the course of billions of galaxies,
unblanketed the birth of space and time.
    We peered to the depths of sacred history,
    examined the fuse where Genesis was lit.
Skilled in excavation, exegesis, we decrypted
    the narrative that nature had concealed in its body.
    We opened the book with ourselves written in it,
became the first listeners to creation's long tale.
    Science rejoined our stories of origin;
    these two estranged brothers met and embraced.
The unexpected heavens uttered our names;
    confronted us anciently with who we are.
    We were held in the grip of searing revelation,
blessed by this sudden magnitude of news,
    and we listened in the muteness of any new wonder,
    the first humans stitched back to the universe's body.
Told that Krishna has eaten dirt,
    Yashoda orders the cheeky boy
    to open his mouth. And there in that glistening
pink cave, where there should be only his miniature
    teeth, the gloss of gums and soft animal of tongue—
    nebulae are mapped on an expanse of black,
the great spirals and rings of galaxies spread,
    and there sparkles the whole music of space and time:
    a night sky replete with stars beyond stars,
extending in magnificent, infinite breadth.
    She's among the billions upon billions of worlds.
    No one has prepared her for what spreads before her.
There, she discerns, is the sun, the Earth—
    she is propelled toward what she sees—
    there the wedge of land where she lives,

        there river, villages, the map of her life.
            And there Yashoda, shaken, sees herself,
            sees herself peering into Krishna's mouth—
she's the theatre where the story faces itself,
            the mirror within the heart of all things.
            She knows that she is here as the guardian
not only of her adopted scallywag son
            but somehow in him of everything that is.
            He is Vishnu, Vishnu is him.
He is not a speck of dust less than everything.
            He embodies as one of the secrets of his being
            the cosmos that pulses and pirouettes before her.
Yashoda is compressed and expanded and wrung
            into nothing in this vision that reduces her to everything
            that is. She blinks, steps back, Krishna closes his mouth.
The universe is before her in human form,
            in inconceivable condensation of scale,
            everything crammed into this boy's small mouth.
She stares at his smirking unfantastic face,
            at the one whose mind holds the stars in place,
            at the lips where creation first whispered itself.

## 7. Becoming Ourselves

The making persists in inviting, alluring us
to become the fantastic beasts of ourselves;
to be phrases by which it writes its way forward,
minor miracles of slim particular lives.
Here we sit, dandled on the lap of time,
born to what slides beneath us, singing.

We hover above the lithe living darkness,
the river-black blood, that we peer down on
and slip ourselves into. Spirits instill us
with specific hungers—allotting us each
some seminal inheritance of sacred history,
some weaving of our temperaments with the ribbons of this world.

Beauty's drawn, black ink, on the backs of our being,
a corporeal keenness animates our days,
a telluric truth lovely in every mineral of our blood.
This body is where the cosmos writes its wish list,
and we crave to live so fearfully doused with light,
to mold what our flesh configures of magnificence.

There are days when we breach from the quotidian
to the densest chroma we've known ourselves to be,
our true clothing descending, gold leaves on our skin,
and the whole long-grieving tree of our desires
shattering its weighted winter darkness to white.
We hear notes that strike us to our own florescence,

are networked in all the tungsten of our veins;
are arrayed for these moments in the clear light of angels
and face the night-black treasures of ourselves.
Rinsed of the accumulated dust of our days,
we are here with perfect pitch for wishes
and pledge ourselves to the intimate Earth.

## 8. Muhammad Heals the Moon

Muhammad faces the fractured moon,
    the midden-ready plate of its face.
    He does not indulge in the plunge to despair
or pause to eulogize these precious fragments.
    He knows this would be a betrayal of story,
    consign him to a poverty he's not willing to endure.
Muhammad is fervently a man of religion:
    of memory flung hard, impassioned, toward hope.
    He pictures what is not, pictures the perfect circle
of the moon, presses its image cool white on his eyes.
    He would heal jagged cracks to clean circumference,
    mold severed matter back to bright sphere.
He prays that its scraps may be fused into one:
    that scattered archipelago of white and wound
    returning to the gravity bred in its bones.
He watches the slow-motion miracle of the moon's
    concrescence as edge is drawn to edge, is sealed,
    until every sliver is deep at home
and a disc of wonder blesses the sky.
    The moon again glides gravid with light,
    drawing our blood and the planet's dark waters.
We moved again through the marvelous foreign,
    encountered and conversed with those rooted elsewhere,
    were balanced by hemispheres not of our birth.
We softened to each other the borders of our skin,
    discovered, with daring, polyamorous delight,
    the polymorphously permeable cultures of Earth.
Women shifted their weight within the world,
    tilted our species toward some balance.
    The starkness of genders eased in our minds,
and we felt ourselves loosened, dangerous with experiment,
    freed to forbidden portions of the palette;
    licked by new fluidity of identity, a queer
willingness to admit what we had not been.
    What made us different made us whole.
    There irrupted some surge toward synthesis—

a place where edges meet, are healed.
    We saw Earth as a floating marble in space,
    saw it precious, wondrous, home,
and we in that image were sphered into one.
    New bodies softened the edges of our scriptures;
    new chapters of salvation blossomed in our days.
We reached for colors ground in all the pestles of the world,
    hungered to be planted with unnative seeds,
    to lift the world's voice in some broader chorus.
Here was the densest we'd known of polyphony;
    here story with story was free to breed.
    We listened to the dissonances of which we're composed,
and all that was alien granted us its blessing.
    We entered some multiply religious procession
    with Vishnu and all his team of comrades,
with Buddha and Jesus and each candescent mystic.
    We glimpsed a fire around which a circle
    of the holy ones sits, the saints and the seers,
the troupe of visionaries, incarnations, the council
    of all the assembled and brightly dressed holy.
    We eavesdropped on conversations among the divine,
imagined a wholeness where there had been only shards.
    We were swathed in all the planet's soft cloth,
    and nursed on the cosmos, conceiving it whole.

## 9. A Tapestry Is Laid over the World

The human world netted itself in sound,
    heard voices and music broadcast from afar,
    huddled round the warmth of a case full of magic;
propelled voices on wires newly strung across the globe,
    made the absent vividly, synthetically present,
    tightened the threads that stitched the continents.
We watched in our homes the daily film of the planet,
    sat transfixed before serial episodes of fictions
    and the million tiny dramas that tugged at our desires.
We were meshed within elaborate textiles,
    this opalescent membrane of human fabrication,
    this tapestry of previously unknown relations.
We learned to set code within the miniscule,
    to ramify the binary to majestic complexity;
    and the digital flooded into our days,
sheathing and sheeting the world we had known.
    It brought the bounty of multiplying minds,
    enhanced the velocities of science and research.
Triumphant with the sudden acceleration of knowledge,
    we hurled ourselves into the future of our species,
    skywalked through the bazaars of the globe.
We took on the attributes, accents of our machines,
    those marvelous prosthetics adept in friendliness,
    slick in seduction, and bearing the amnesia
of what our species before them had been.
    We drifted in diffuse encyclopedic knowledge,
    a blizzard of data buffeted our days,
a welter of information, mercantilism, sleaze,
    diversion and insidious misinformation.
    Everyone was instantly as proximate as our thumbs,
and all knowledge, it seemed, was conjurable by digits,
    by the carillon and the illuminated texts,
    the glowing psalters we held in our hands.
Attention weakened with the onslaught of impulse,
    and we became inseparable from our machines,
    creatures who tap and scan and swipe.

Enchanted, we permitted the excision of soil
    and silence from our lives, the retreat of nature
    from the screens of our senses; we turned from the fabulous
beauties of the world to where we might live
    with all our eyes closed. We held to the pyxes
    of our devices, slid to the most designed of addictions.
The striders across a wondrous frontier,
    the keepers of unaccountable knowledge,
    we wandered lost in the glowing wood of our lives.
A widow wishes to fashion a simulacrum of the world,
    a depiction of paradise stitched by human hands,
    a summoning of bright aspirations to a tapestry.
Visited by a vision of what her life might be,
    and captivated by the reach of her consummate craft,
    she is driven to trade years of her life for its making.
She hurries to the market, procures the threads
    dyed in every corner of the Earth: gold
    and silver, lapis and violet, saffron
and vermilion, the notes of every species of flower.
    She seats herself before her loom, given over
    to the fingering and looping of hues, this delight.
She cannot shift her sight from loom to world
    and back, from realm to realm. She does not pause
    to sell her work, to buy rice, to cook,
immured in the myopic crafting of her hands.
    Her eyes fixed on the screen of the tapestry before her,
    this work that absorbs the hours of her nights,
her tears of salt and tears of blood,
    she constructs a world pearled within the world.
    She hears the notes of each tint she touches,
and her senses shimmer on the nerves of the threads.
    She finishes this work of surpassing wonder,
    lays it as her legacy upon a breathing field.
On the grass it is stirred by a beckoning breeze
    that quickens and animates each of its fibers,
    until her tapestry, the site of her afflatus, toil,
this fresh skin placed on the skin of the world,
    spreads out toward every line of horizon,
    blankets and replaces all the land in sight.

### 10. Snow White and We Keep Hankering for More

We craved the cowries and bibelots of status,
    the objects that solaced and satined our days,
    chasing stray flags of gadget and fashion;
were convinced of the common good of acquisition,
    the ways it must accrue to the worth of the world.
    We took our measure by the finesse of our consumption,
succumbed to the insidious infestation of our eyes,
    cultivated proclivities the planet could not bear,
    cracked the bones of our home to squeeze out more
pleasure, our sight constricted by what we still coveted.
    Adjacent to the millions who hungered for grain,
    we constructed our mountains and monuments of waste.
We stood indicted by the avarice of our lives,
    by these charms that dwelt so close to our hearts,
    charms that we would not barter for a future.
Snow White has an eye for, desires, the pretty,
    deserves more than the penniless dwarves can provide.
    Their injunction for her preservation is clear:
she must not ever admit a peddler.
    But here, in a hue that unlocks her cache of dopamine,
    are the exquisite, lovely laces for her bodice
arrayed in the royal peddler's hand.
    Snow White cannot resist. They're a treat,
    an indulgence, a benediction on her day.
The queen, assisting her, tightens the strings
    of the girl's suffocation. Snow White is lying
    breathless on the floor when the little men come home.
They loosen the laces, unstrangle all her organs.
    She regains her breath, tells them that she
    simply could not say no. The orders
are repeated to her, slowly. The queen returns
    in a new peddler's outfit, tempts Snow White
    with the glamour of a comb, its exclusive elegance
adorning her hair, rendering her royal, stellar,
    a figure exalted to someone far exceeding
    herself. Snow White assents, her heart

a flurry, a whirligig, a craving for makeover.
    The queen strokes her tresses, stabs the comb to her scalp—
    poison sharp in its every tine.
Again Snow White collapses to the floor,
    lies as a splendidly elegant corpse:
    her vanity the target any archer can strike.
The dwarves unfork the comb, tell her again.
    But their warnings can't annul the desires of her eyes.
    She is starkly immune to admonition,
to threat and all that dull talk of consequence.
    The peddler returns. Here again is the apple,
    fresh in its marriage of goodness and harm.
The queen touts the fruit's incontestable merits,
    its perfection, its sweetness, attests that she
    never passes a day without taking one.
The queen eats. Snow White eats. Snow White falls.
    What she is glutted with lodges in her throat,
    holds her to the floor and the coffin of coma.
She like fruit is left to rot.
    The squirrel-like dwarves circle round her, perplexed.
    Birds chitter about her mute, hungry beauty.
She lies as a testament to the innocence of greed,
    the wondrously sympathetic desire for goods,
    the ingenuous candor of just wanting more.

## 11. The Earth Is Threatened and We Foresee Our Destruction

Indignant Diana splashes live water
    in Actaeon's face. She will not be subject to his lust,
    her flesh laid bare on the couch of his retina.
With those drops he pours to a fluid becoming,
    his body lengthening, furring, thickening with muscle,
    showered with stature, gravity, grace,
granted the unthinking perfection of animal limbs,
    this new mass he maneuvers with instinctive skill.
    He leaps from inside this new majesty of flesh,
a fitting new armature balanced on his head,
    an ornate candelabra of weaponry and pride,
    and he is all poise in each lift to air.
He knows in his hugeness a new scent of fear,
    a shiver that ripples through each alert fiber—
    and newly embodied, he tastes his own blood.
He is a beauty inviting teeth. He
    hears the baying and howling of hounds
    that in his lost life were the sounds
of his own thoughts sprinting through the forest.
    His companions, these dogs who were the sleek
    agents of his will, in an instant have circled
in a betrayal he does not know the spell to reverse.
    He stinks with the musk, the panic of his fear.
    The eyes of those who adored him
are filled with a glinting yellow violence.
    A phalanx of teeth hurls snarling through the air
    in the silver running sweat of his fear,
this fear that is his only essence and name,
    the frenzy of having in his body nowhere to flee,
    no voice to call off his ravaging hounds.
He is the terror of the dogs he has mastered,
    the prey of his own vision and voice:
    he is their only tutor in carnage.
His body is ripped in electric pain,
    gouged by mouths tearing flank and throat—
    and his own dogs—his beloved, faithful dogs.

Human population swelled exponentially,
    straining the load on the land that would support us.
    We fed ourselves, clothed ourselves, amassed our possessions,
chased from their homes the world's other creatures.
    Earth dwindled to a thinner band of life,
    and we marked the years of accelerating erasure,
when every few minutes bleeped another extinction:
    Caribbean monk seal, Caspian tiger,
    Eskimo curlew, golden toad,
Pyrenean ibex, Western black rhinoceros,
    baiji river dolphin, the blanks and the blanks,
    the zodiac of loss beneath which we lived.
We heard the litanies of our vanishing species
    and numbered the hundreds we had never learned.
    We consigned to the fabular all that is not us
or those species conscripted to provide us with food.
    The animals we named in childhood faded,
    leaving their holes in our mouths and our minds,
folding forever the hands of their futures,
    their copious codices of epiphany and gene.
    We heard the loss and our hearts iced over,
eyes frozen with tears we could not weep.
    We ruled over sere depauperate land,
    the seas' munificence stripped to near death.
We moved from one ruined species to the next,
    forgot that the brilliant blood of the world
    flowed like the nectar of stars in our veins.
We scrumped from the only garden that could feed us.
    We made commerce of the organs of Earth,
    pillaged the innards of this generous planet,
burned it with pyromaniac pleasure,
    enlarged our perverse panoply of disposable toys;
    corrupted the ground, our source and sustenance,
trashed and heated the waters from which we arose,
    choked and stuffed the air with our fumes.
    We steered the weather rudely from its course,
twisting the dials we had no power to reverse,
    inviting to our planet dark angels and plagues:
    drought and famine, wildfire and flood,

the slewing contradictions and disruptions of order.
    We quaffed the milk of unborn generations,
    catastrophe inconceivable in the comfort of our days.
We wished to duck our heads from knowledge,
    assure ourselves that nothing in our days need change.
    Now, as we stagger, set upon by hounds,
we slide toward a suicide the Earth will bear with us.
    Built to be in love with the world,
    we begin to admit that the world is ill,
that we have poisoned the one who sustains us.
    And we are here, in these days of paralysis,
    this conundrum of knowing what we do not live.
We have no more than an unzealous wish
    for the Earth's preservation. We wonder and grieve
    how this came to be, how this can be so.
Phaethon, a youth of uncertain paternity,
    is told that the sun god is his own father,
    that the whole Apollonian heritage is his.
The boy requires proof of who he is
    and climbs to the house of the sun, intoxicated
    by the opulence of Apollo's carved palace,
by marble and ivory and elaborate craft,
    by radiance that dazzles his human eyes.
    The most refulgent of gods receives him,
and he hears Apollo call him, unabashedly, son,
    basks in his lineage, senses ichor in his veins.
    And as a means of weighting his word,
Apollo vows to grant him any wish he picks.
    Humans are not fashioned to endure such indulgence,
    have bones that crack beneath such a burden.
Phaethon blurts out what he's barely contained
    in his mouth, this craving and obsession that has festered
    in his mind for months: to drive his father's
stallions through the wide reeling sky;
    to be the one who shapes the course of the sun
    and metes out the heat for each kingdom on Earth.
Apollo, frozen on the web of his granted wish,
    entreats Phaethon to relent, to choose more prudently,
    to turn from this task that taxes even Apollo's prowess,

to match his request to the skill of his hand.
>    But Phaethon can find no listening in his body,
>    lusts in his hands for mastery of the heavens.
Apollo cannot unspeak his promise,
>    hitches the fierce stamping steeds to the car,
>    counsels Phaethon to follow the medial path,
to run equidistant between heaven and Earth.
>    Phaethon, eager, untutored, is off.
>    The gates of dawn purple and rose the way before him,
and he basks in a perfect, exalted moment
>    of glory, holding the reins and coursing in the sky,
>    the wind in his hair as if it worships him.
But his are not the imagined arms of a god;
>    he has not the adroitness, the muscle, the will;
>    the horses sense his greenness and will not be steered,
he veers from the tracks in the road of the sky,
>    arcs too high and singes the heavens—
>    the wide constellations are unstuck by heat,
bears and serpents routing in terror.
>    Phaethon stares panicked to the mirror of his presumption,
>    flails, calls out, racing blankness in place
of the horses' names; his lips and hands useless
>    as they clutch at the reins, at the words, as they fail.
>    He careens and grazes the dry skin of Earth,
abrades the land he had sought to soar over.
>    He watches the torching of the patient year's harvest,
>    fields grayed to smoke and ash beneath him.
He feels the map of his own brain burning,
>    the arteries inside him scorched to desert.
>    Fish are stewed within their waters,
the currents of water and wind are stirred
>    to scribbles, peaks of ice shed their statuary white,
>    lakes and rivers vanishing to steam,
ocean creeping higher up the calves of the land.
>    The soil cracks itself to pottery's dryness,
>    wastelands spread fingers over wide continents.
Phaethon cannot endure the ovening heat.
>    Gaia herself, the primal unvocal goddess
>    of Earth, is singed in her eyebrows and flowing hair,

rails at this payment for her cyclic fertility,
    her openhanded generosity to all who are hers.
    Gaia, indignant, roused from her sibilance
to wail, ululation, ferocious rebuke,
    cries out to Olympus, to Zeus and all
    the lofty and idle and governing gods,
that the perpetrator of this abomination
    must be brought down; that this indignity, this outrage,
    this flagrant assault on life must be stopped.

## 12. Praise

We are breathless with praise and its failing.
Might we be able to praise the pivot,
the plucking of ripe, unsatiating fruit,

the welding in a single rapacious act
of the world's advancement and its corruption?
And what of our compression to cities, nations,

our assembly to some jerried resurrected bird?
We cannot praise the history of betrayal,
honor the slavery, the chicanery of Jacob,

the pillage of body, language, land.
We are left with lacunae in praise,
abysses where it cannot rightly be spoken.

We are left with only moth-eaten praise.
We praise the unearthing of ancient story,
the disclosure of metamorphosis in the species of the Earth,

Raven's thrilled discovery of, fiddling with his mask;
praise the plunging of telling to earliest origin,
the recitation of the tale of the thousand creations,

the myriad revelations in the body of the cosmos,
the descending divinities who remind us who we are,
the universe swirling in a boy's stretching mouth.

We praise the gift of a sweet swelling narrative
where time is unbroken, möbiused with myth,
and gods are wondrously resident on Earth.

We marvel at the generously extended hand
that beckons us toward some extension of history,
invites us to enstory the wishes of the world.

We praise the meeting of the edges of the foreign,
the fertilization of every alterity,
the union of the shattered splinters of the moon.

We might praise the florescence of human tools,
the tendrils extending across the planet,
the graceful silk of our intimate liaisons.

And we lament the loss of the world on which
they're laid, the amnesia, the occlusion of beauty,
the distraction, agitation, which infest our days.

We cannot finagle our way to the praise of greed—
our alacrity to join the queue of the suicides,
to sacrifice our existence for one more indulgence.

We cannot praise the splash of reversal,
the moment our snarling hounds encircle us,
the prospect of a death of our own manufacture.

Nothing on Earth could stand further from praise
than our merciless stripping of animal life,
our impassive decimation of our sentient kin,

our insouciant scarring of this planet's features,
this violation that appalls the staring stars.
Phaethon hurls us to the utter obscenity

of praise, plunges us down to the pit of lament,
the conflagration of all the magnanimous Earth.
As we look full in the face of disaster,

the unravelling of what the cosmos has crafted,
we cannot, still, do other than praise.
We praise the finely crazed beauty of Earth:

the stars that still cupola themselves on our nights,
the lit green that beglamours the tips of our leaves,
the glinting of strewn gold in the dust of our days.

*Seven*

## 1. Listening

We return to this particular clearing in history,
the caesura of listening where we began—

this silver field of silence where the coming
might be heard. We listen to the clarion

stillness at the center of our flesh. We would,
for all the world, continue, follow a bright path

leading green through the trees, trace
the inscriptions we find written on the cosmos—

that something of promise might sit adjacent
to every previewed scene of extinction.

Always this thirsting world wants for its singing
all that envelops us, and also, inexplicably,

us. We listen as if listening were our purest name,
as if this were the reason we are here;

listen for susurration that stirs beneath
our hearing; for the moment when from blank

interregnum lifts lilt and sonority of song.
We listen for a further epic, scripture,

a further phase of Vishnu's dreams,
for the breath of the beloved as it moves on our face.

We listen for ancient ways that might coax us
toward the tableaux of a faceable future;

we listen for the florilegium of stories
by which we might yet find our way;

for the scenes, the lines, the verbal stirrings
that would pierce our novice hearts with light.

## 2. The Lost Disciples Find Their Way

Jesus is dead. Two disciples are walking
    when a third man joins the leaderless travelers
    on the road. He asks for their news, hears
a word about Jesus, perorates upon the one
    they have lost, spirits them through an exegesis
    of scripture, granting his footfalls of light
to their history, recounting long stories
    that loop through each other, patterns and fractals
    that hum in their skulls, buffing dull texts
so they gleam in his hands, excavating the fossils
    secreted in the prophets, stringing them together
    into some scintillating, life-turning tale.
The stranger has found Jesus in all the blind history
    that preceded him; zoomed out from the frame,
    set sidereal order on the events of their lives.
He's wandered among their unordered scriptures
    with a magnet, elicited there what had been
    invisible, faceted and polished passages to shine
with new dream-tones of light. The disciples are enlisted
    in a narrative they thought they'd outlived, and they find
    salvation in this stitching of sacred antecedents
like a lining to their lives, their own placement
    at the forward edge of history, this
    turning toward a freshly sown future.
This man has disturbed none of the facts they knew
    but braided them into a sudden new story.
    The disciples are swept up with his stirring speech,
enchanted by the mythic world he's unearthed.
    They hunger to extend their time in his telling,
    to inhabit this narrative as if it were their lives.
They press him to linger, share their simple dinner,
    and his words blessing bread are unmistakable
    in cadence, in timbre and tone, in some sensuous
coursing of welcome, forgiveness, love.
    Jesus? they stammer. With the name
    he is gone. They grasp at the fabric

of an afternoon's memory, recall how their hearts
    were ablaze with his words. They are again bereft
    of their beloved; but now they are endowed
with a lineage, the rippling fabric of inheritance.
    They are dumbfoundingly bequeathed with a commission:
    they are the keepers and continuers of this story.
Here where our world might be given up for lost,
    the story shoulders in, commandeers our lives,
    enlists us as the unlikely amanuenses of this Earth.
And we begin to live with ears alert
    for words that match and mend our days.
    We listen to this brilliance that envelops us,
that needs us to provide the next unwritten page,
    leaves no one but us to blaze its way forward.
    The thread that appeared to abandon us has not,
and we are here in these delicate days
    that are the tumulus or reignition of our lives.
    We are left with the bodily imprint of a story
visited upon us like religious vocation—
    a commission that fits cleanly with everything we are
    and plainly exceeds any talents we've been granted.
The making will not leave us here unstoried,
    marooned without something akin to tale.
    And what would our conversion be
but this to new scripture, new poetry, new song,
    to the sweet continuance of the making of the world?
    And this work I hold no credential to take part in?
One that was given me ritually in dream,
    shown by some summoning foreman of spirits.
    The task: to fill these small set panels
left blank in the book; to illuminate
    only these numbered pages of manuscript,
    a patient scriptorium at labor around me.

### 3. Moses and We Meet the Holy World

There, on another pedestrian shepherding day,
    a rote day beaded on the twine of his life,
    Moses strides among the dry wilderness of hours.
He is accosted by a brandishing brush of flame,
    a refulgence blazing at the center of his vision,
    what was bush now assaulting, overwhelming his sight.
He has never seen anything as dazzling as this—
    light like a tear in the texture of the world.
    It trips all the idling toy soldiers of his mind.
Moses is transfixed by this ambush of radiance,
    lit as a wildfire at the base of his brain.
    He stands before the rippling furnace of the world—
and what can he do but cast off all
    the sandals of his mind? He stands
    before the world stripped to its electric skin,
feels its current white in all the branchwork of his brain,
    faces holiness where he had seen only dull scrub.
    The language he knows is no match for this.
Here is voice that is the voice of this world,
    a raw eruption from the cellar beneath
    his speech, voice that shimmers and slips
to absolute being. Moses becomes before this bush
    a man eviscerated, a man of religion:
    human mouth before all this enveloping beauty.
He witnesses the flow of gold and copper,
    the ferocious, fluttering voice of flame,
    the melting metals of this purest world.
For moments too silver and mercurial
    to hold, we know this bright cosmos, this surging
    procession of mystery, florescence, as one
flashing river of intimate voice, as this
    great and gracious arc of acts, the whole
    rattling tale of coruscant creation. Who is
this flow of fire whom we have watched
    in its long cascading phases of creation;
    who invites us to be present when foundations are laid,

whose late love is this great breach of secrets?
    Who is this enigma assembled all of entry,
       this thrum of becoming at the base of each day?
Motes of millennia have nested in our lives,
    and when we again address the making,
    we know it as the supple genius of the story,
know it as listener and lover and lord,
    as creation still boisterous with its wish to compose;
    know it too as the destitute weltering body
of this world, as grief inscribed upon our flesh.
    We remember with glistening our lineage in beauty,
    in the hopes of this holy material world,
in some line of listening that cannot be cut.
    We see how our lives might be stitched
    back to the bowl and the birth of the stars,
the breadth of creation in our time and in time.
    And we know beyond our known religions
    the sheerly religious disclosure of the cosmos.
We wake within this great metamorphosis,
    this story from which we have never been exiled,
    that is the revelation, the invocation of our lives.

## 4. Communion

We have tracked the attraction of atoms, pullulation
of seas, the glissando of sentience through animal
flesh. We have watched ourselves shifting
through phases of our story, known other eyes
gazing out from the world—that instant when the stag
appeared facing me at dusk, niched in his clearing,

bearer of news. We have known the clicking
of switches across the kingdoms, felt our edges
soften beyond borders of species. We have beheld
the world that, with us, beholds us; we have
been welcomed as members of the assembly of animal
saints. We have known that if we opened our lips

we'd be choir—that for all our aloneness
wholeness is home. We return to that circle
where we span the bodies of countless creatures
and the holy excludes no figures we've known.
No one is here save the oldest magic:
the wishing, the dreaming, the conjuring from flame.

In this hatching of ourselves toward all imagined light,
in what we in our splendid vernacular call prayer,
magnitude courses through the scrim of our skin,
and the purest nature of what we've called cosmos
is not matter or motion, particle or pattern,
but communion bright in their disguise.

## 5. Gautama and the Signs of Turning

His years turn, well oiled, on the wheel of their pleasures,
    unclouded by any unsightly decay,
    until the day Prince Gautama rides
with his driver forbiddenly beyond the palace.
    The road is unmanicured, potholed, jars
    the riders; plants, ungardened, grown rank, misshapen;
refuse has been left to spoil and reek. Gautama
    is assaulted by elements all out of place, does
    not recognize this world as the world.
Here is an old man, the wires of his body
    arthritically tightened; depleted, skeletal,
    bubbling in the shallow waters of senescence.
Here is a sick man, Job-covered with boils,
    pain infecting his every wincing motion,
    eyes narrowed to the scrabbling reach for relief.
The prince is not himself but terror, upheaval.
    He wells with a foreign cast of emotions:
    alarm, revulsion, incredulity, and
the thread of some thin trickling compassion.
    He wants to flee and wake up in his life,
    ensconced in the timeless time of the palace.
Laid out like the obsidian tableau of a dream,
    bewildering, abhorrent, a turmoil of flies,
    a man diminished to the rotting of flesh.
What is this? pleads Gautama,
    sheeting his nose and his mouth with his sleeve.
    Death has already invaded his nostrils;
what he sees cannot be skimmed from his life.
    He is adrift in the limbo of this moment,
    cannot retreat to his sybaritic days.
There, in the midst of this pitch of suffering,
    is a man who does not avert his face from it,
    who is some walking pain of peace,
whose life is an alien realm—a monk.
    Gautama begs from his eyes: this man who is apostate
    to all the indulgence Gautama holds dear.

He is not the answer, does not hold
    the answer, and his gaze untethers all Gautama's
    confusions. The prince is ruined by what
he has met; he cannot creep back to the man
    he has been, cannot sequester this day in his brain.
    He cannot opt for the smaller of knowledges.
It is a day to which we wish we had not woken.
    The signs have displayed themselves, preempted
    old directions. And we are sorely
nostalgic for ignorance, grieve the lives
    we'd enjoy without this disclosure. Our old
    world has crumpled, burning paper in our hands.
We have witnessed heatwaves, wildfires, floods;
    seen the melting of glaciers, calving of icecaps,
    the graphs that chart the planet's fever.
We have known dire prophecies encroach on our days.
    And we stand in a strangely vacant conversion:
    relinquishing our lovely untenable lives;
knowing only a blur of future before us.
    It is not something we would wish on anyone.
    We press our ears to the lips of this Earth,
find not hope but hope in hope's existence.
    We attempt to believe, in the deadest of days,
    that creation is still where our hearts are home,
where our first, our only allegiance lies.
    And we are late and damage has been done.
    We are awash in inchoate wishes:
that we might live religiously here;
    that compassion might inhabit the sparseness of our hearts;
    that the future will not leave us here unvocationed.
We wish for a trueing of the compass of our lives:
    that we might not persist inimical to Earth
    but fall back to love with this long-suffering world.

## 6. Hanuman Discovers a Way to Continue

We balance here on the cusp of history,
    with no sure knowledge of what is to come,
    scout for routes which are ours to trace.
If there is some way for us to proceed,
    it might be upon the footpaths of our stories,
    upon the old wishes engraved on this world.
Ancient tales drift like snow on our lives,
    shimmer and sparkle with native invitation
    to press ourselves deeply to the days of the making.
Our bodies abuzz with what is unbroken,
    we glimpse a shadowed door that admits us,
    elicit from darkness a nod to step forward.
We remember this one, an exemplum of devotion,
    who will not acquiesce to the death of his lord;
    who lives with us in meager unsufficing knowledge.
With Hanuman, we scan the field where Rama—
    his beloved, his adored, the blue lord enthroned
    in the shrine of his heart—lies dead: victim
of the strafe of snakes shot by invisible
    archers in the sky; snakes that have suffocated
    the beautiful body of Rama. Before Hanuman,
the vista of untellably bereft and barren years.
    The monkey-king weeps for the loss of this man,
    all meaning with Rama drained from his days,
every reverence bleached from his flesh.
    And Hanuman is told, extravagantly, by the voice
    of a vulture, a voice that fantasticates on the world
as it is, that there is still for lifeless Rama
    a cure: one rare species of alpine flower
    that secretes the power to restore him to life:
a blue flower shaped precisely so, with this
    exact unmistakable chroma; only its unique aroma
    can save him. It is a hope as frail as a fairy tale,
a hope less sound than simple despair. Hanuman
    swats a thousand doubts from his mind,
    propels himself to swift ascent, catapulting

to the mountaintop, every weary branch of his life
    on fire. He searches for a floral exactitude
    that eludes him. The mountain is strewn with a palette
of beguiling flowers all slightly at odds:
    gentian, cornflower, lapis, cerulean,
    all those day and dusking shades of blue
in geometries of infinitely minor variations,
    kaleidoscoping with each slight shift of the breeze.
    Bewildered by all the codes of color at the summit
of the world, he rings with the clapper of his bitter
    stupidity, and in every direction he turns is loss:
    salvation within reach and he cannot find it.
The meadow will not simplify itself toward cure,
    and Hanuman wants—wants more than his own
    pulsing life—wants the life of his world
to go on. He will not do nothing. In a fit
    of furious aggrieved adoration he tears
    from its shoulders the peak of the mountain,
snaps off what must encompass the unfindable flower,
    lifts the mountaintop like a waiter's tray,
    skis down the great canted slopes of the sky,
circles and censers the peak over Rama's cadaver,
    cloaking the battlefield in a blue blur of light.
    Tendrils of scent waft to the smooth, soon-quivering
nostrils of Rama, enter the temples of Rama's lungs
    that swell with that supernal hue; the scent infuses
    his blood, renews his life. The perfume of a flower
restores the great warrior, permits the paused, hopeless
    world to resume. Hanuman watches
    as his history, that had closed, revives;
watches as Rama, the adored, the one body of his world,
    opens eyelids, shakes off snakes,
    rises in azure to the next of his lives.

## 7. Gods Make a New Deity

We stand vigil through this night of meteoric destruction,
    weathering the long malediction of weather,
    clutching tiny seeds of rebirth in our fists.
We pluck what we can from the dark sack
    of prophecy, embarking with our indigenous ignorance
    to the dimly lit, demanding next page of the tale.
We approach with no less than everything we know:
    every gleaned and rummaged scrap of wisdom,
    each ingredient that might be of conceivable use.
There is no minor niche in our pantheon,
    no backbench deity we could exclude
    in the attempt to fashion some makeshift future
from the ragbag of ill-matched goods at hand.
    We need nothing less than the endlessly generative
    grammar of the cosmos, its traditions of wonder,
its profusion of characters, storylines, scenes,
    that we might be exceeded by what is to come,
    by the breeding and ferocious re-creation of the sacred.
A demon is ravaging the creatures of the Earth.
    The remnant people and animals are cowed;
    the gods huddled on a narrow and dizzying
precipice; they are not adequate to this crushing crisis.
    The gods themselves are in need of salvation.
    There is nothing to be done but attempt to engender
new deity—fusing, surpassing individual magics.
    The gods bubble with speculation at what
    is beyond them, offer their desperate unanimous
contributions of themselves, each one emitting
    some essence, some singular liquid power
    to add to the pot. They watch in hope
the convergence of a thousand smaller intentions,
    scent the aroma of all their old fortunes combined
    in the nebular swirling of ejaculate light.
And for some course of time there is nothing:
    everything proffered, no one revealed;
    they have issued a coin that holds no face.

She comes when she is beckoned by the wishes of
    the world: the darling of all their jostling devotions.
    She is a listening from before she was born,
a sport that elaborates the lineage of gods,
    her body built of spit and aspiration.
    She colludes with all that is wondrous in this world,
breaks herself open like a scepter of light—
    all the progeny the gods ever feared to conceive.
    She strikes stark terror in the hearts of her makers.
She is an amalgam of melted divinities,
    the emission of multiple sacred mouths,
    a holy composed of uncountable holies,
a figure of tremendous and terrifying beauty,
    a goddess with a wingspan that leaves the gods
    agape. She arrives with a fierce revanchist will
and all the gradations of polygamous birth.
    She commits the delicious inverse of suicide:
    assaults the one who would smother life,
tears like an animal's tonsils and tongue
    the demon's hot life from the purse of its flesh,
    leaves its steaming carcass seeping to soil.
She sutures the thinning frayed skin of the world,
    breathes, in her stunning aftermath, peace,
    makes the broad land again haven and home.

## 8. Varaha Rescues the Still Beautiful Earth

We would sing and keep singing through the years of burning
    while arrows of fire sebastian our flesh—
    that singing might loose the grip of death,
lead us to some realm where story can continue.
    We listen for a myth that is languishing and thirsting
    for our lives, drawing us like some long-neglected
music that bids us to walk with joy
    in the rivers, the mirrors of this world. We would turn
    within that flash of silver, imagine ourselves
as the Buddhas and Vishnus and bright Christs
    of our day, who step to Earth to restore it
    to rightness, tireless inside the work of their lives.
Ambushed by our love for a world we had shunned,
    we're enticed to this raggedly beautiful planet,
    its magnificence that persists despite its destitution.
And here again we listen for Vishnu
    as he plunges to depths for his love of the Earth—
    lit by the marvel of his own making.
Another demon has strip-mined the features of Earth,
    pocked her face with moon-like marks,
    siphoned the liquids from within her pierced veins.
Earth has come unstuck from her orbit,
    tossed from her lofty height to drown
    in the waters that fester on the cosmos's floor.
Vishnu from his heaven sights this atrocity,
    quickly flicks through the racks and hangers of his wardrobe,
    holds up to his God-form a costume
all urgency, ferality, and tusks, fills it
    with the snorting hot breath of God:
    Vishnu the dreamer now Varaha the boar.
He is maddened in every keen craving tissue,
    magnified by all that he scents and seeks,
    bristling and itching with physical want,
sweating with the sweet saturation of desire.
    He forks and hurls himself like lightning,
    hurtling down the speeding trafficway of sky,

plunges to the gelid black waters of death.
    His breath is held like a stopwatch inside him.
    For time he is lost without sense or direction.
In black chaos he finds the sphere he has sought
    and plucks her as an ardent prince hefts a princess,
    lifts the Earth-goddess softly on his tusks,
raises her, bedraggled, from the waters of her ruin.
    She is guttered and yet not robbed of the exquisite,
    holds in her wreckage residual glory.
He is ravished by the ravaged body of the Earth,
    his heart racing at a pace he had not envisaged,
    his body astonished by her driven beauty.
Vishnu the creator is stung by the loveliness
    his own mind, his breath, his dream has made,
    is grateful that he did not dawdle in heaven.
He beholds her and love poems foam inside him
    in this maelstrom where his divinity is reordered
    by what he adores; some gold at his center
melted and molded for the first time in his lives.
    He swoons with the dizzying tilt of his axis,
    flings open the unknown mansions of his heart,
exalts her as bright holiness freshly discovered.
    He succumbs to this merging devotion to the world
    and rings with the truest note of himself,
the blue that utters him, time before time;
    is flooded with rapture as the newest of his names.
    He wants only to save her and save her
while eternity drifts—pool and pearl
    and blue silk garments. And she, who is seen,
    accepts his outspoken prodigality of love,
glows as the one the creator forever adores.
    He returns her to the fine silver wire of her orbit
    where her flesh commences its long lovely return,
renews the profusion of what was shorn from her;
    where she rebuilds the slow charms of her sensuous life
    and circles in the spacious love of her star.

## 9. Praise

Praise what has carried us from first note to now.
Praise the ouroboros of event and telling,
the twisting helices of human knowing.

Praise the cosmos that reveals itself home of the holy—
tucked beneath the blankets of time and space—
that ignites and incites in us new scripture.

Praise the world that flames its marvels before us,
the Earth ablaze with its daily revelations,
our eyes even fleetingly available to miracle.

Praise the softening of ourselves to our Earthly relations,
our welcome to the making's contemplative life,
the prayer, the communion, that shelters, enfolds us.

Praise Gautama's venturing beyond his father's walls,
his accostal by what he does not wish to see,
the willingness to submit to the sacrifice of turning.

Praise Hanuman in his unbridled devotion,
his keenness to leap to unknowable salvation,
his impulsion to revive the beloved of his heart.

Praise the Goddess concocted from the loss of other options,
the swirling coalescence of the liquids of gods,
the ferocity of the one who restores us to our home.

Praise the ferality and ardor of Varaha
charging to black and unmappable waters,
the maker's seduction by the beauty of Earth.

Praise our entry at this exact seam of story;
the gathering of all the components of the cosmos
into a whole and devotional telling;

the furtherance among us of the one ancient music,
this universe canted to florescence and play,
this singing that becomes both way and wonder.

## 10. Envoi

We have dwelt
              and we have wandered
in the here and hereafter
                      and long herebefore.
The psalms of our history
                    now risen to our lips,
we stand in ornately
              rewritten skin.
May we speak from the billions
                      of years in our mouths;
may we live in listening
              and creation and praise;
may we love this world
              in its storied whole;
may creation's bright voices
                  sing out its names.
Visit on us
        the not yet tellable;
fill the tissues of our hearts
                  with Earthly wishes
that we might be people
                faithful to making.
May we not succumb
                to the snuffing of splendor
but bear the next notes
              of the cosmos's song.
It begins with us
            for the billionth time.
Our listening again
              is where we begin.

www.ingramcontent.com/pod-product-compliance
Lightning Source LLC
Chambersburg PA
CBHW071428160426
43195CB00013B/1841